What readers are saying about
Pragmatic Unit Testing in C#...

"Anybody coding in .NET or, for that matter, any language, would do well to have a copy of this book, not just on their bookshelf, but sitting open in front of their monitor. Unit testing is an essential part of any programmer's skill set, and Andy and Dave have written (yet another) essential book on the topic."

▶ **Justin Gehtland,** Founder, Relevance LLC

"The Pragmatic Programmers have done it again with this highly useful guide. Aimed directly at C# programmers using the most popular unit-testing package for the language, it goes beyond the basics to show what you should test and how you should test it. Recommended for all .NET developers."

▶ **Mike Gunderloy,**
Contributing Editor, ADT Magazine

"As part of the Mono project, we routinely create and maintain extensive unit tests for our class libraries. This book is a fantastic introduction for those interested in creating solid code."

▶ **Miguel de Icaza,** Mono Project, Novell, Inc.

"Andy and Dave have created an excellent, practical and (of course) very pragmatic guide to unit-testing, illustrated with plenty of examples using the latest version of NUnit."

▶ **Charlie Poole,** NUnit framework developer

"Using the approaches described by Dave and Andy you can reduce greatly the number of defects you put into your code. The result will be faster development of better programs. Try these techniques—they will work for you!"

▶ **Ron Jeffries,** www.XProgramming.com

Pragmatic Unit Testing

in C# with NUnit

Pragmatic Unit Testing
in C# with NUnit

Andy Hunt

Dave Thomas

The Pragmatic Bookshelf
Raleigh, North Carolina   Dallas, Texas

Many of the designations used by manufacturers and sellers to distinguish their products are claimed as trademarks. Where those designations appear in this book, and The Pragmatic Programmers, LLC was aware of a trademark claim, the designations have been printed in initial capital letters or in all capitals. The Pragmatic Starter Kit, The Pragmatic Programmer, Pragmatic Programming, Pragmatic Bookshelf and the linking *"g"* device are trademarks of The Pragmatic Programmers, LLC.

Every precaution was taken in the preparation of this book. However, the publisher assumes no responsibility for errors or omissions, or for damages that may result from the use of information (including program listings) contained herein.

Our Pragmatic courses, workshops and other products can help you and your team create better software and have more fun. For more information, as well as the latest Pragmatic titles, please visit us at:

> http://www.pragmaticprogrammer.com

Printed in the United States of America.

ISBN 0-9745140-2-0

Printed on acid-free paper with 85% recycled, 30% post-consumer content.

Second printing, May 2004

Version: 2004-4-22

Contents

About the Starter Kit

Our first book, *The Pragmatic Programmer: From Journeyman to Master*, is a widely-acclaimed overview of practical topics in modern software development. Since it was first published in 1999, many people have asked us about follow-on books, or sequels. We'll get around to that. But first, we thought we'd go back and offer a *prequel* of sorts.

Over the years, we've found that many of our pragmatic readers who are just starting out need a helping hand to get their development infrastructure in place, so they can begin forming good habits early. Many of our more advanced pragmatic readers understand these topics thoroughly, but need help convincing and educating the rest of their team or organization. We think we've got something that can help.

The *Pragmatic Starter Kit* is a three-volume set that covers the essential basics for modern software development. These volumes include the practices, tools, and philosophies that you need to get a team up and running and super-productive. Armed with this knowledge, you and your team can adopt good habits easily and enjoy the safety and comfort of a well-established "safety net" for your project.

Volume I, *Pragmatic Version Control*, describes how to use version control as the cornerstone of a project. A project without version control is like a word processor without an UNDO button: the more text you enter, the more expensive a mistake will be. Pragmatic Version Control shows you how to use version control systems effectively, with all the benefits and safety but without crippling bureaucracy or lengthy, tedious procedures.

This volume, *Pragmatic Unit Testing*, is the second volume in the series. Unit testing is an essential technique as it provides real-world, real-time feedback for developers as we write code. Many developers misunderstand unit testing, and don't realize that it makes *our* jobs as developers easier. This volume is available in two different language versions: in Java with JUnit, and in C# with NUnit.

Volume III, *Pragmatic Automation*,[1] covers the essential practices and technologies needed to automate your code's build, test, and release procedures. Few projects suffer from having too much time on their hands, so Pragmatic Automation will show you how to get the computer to do more of the mundane tasks by itself, freeing you to concentrate on the more interesting—and difficult—challenges.

These books are created in the same approachable style as our first book, and address specific needs and problems that you face in the trenches every day. But these aren't dummy-level books that only give you part of the picture; they'll give you enough understanding that you'll be able to invent your own solutions to the novel problems you face that we *haven't* addressed specifically.

For up-to-date information on these and other books, as well as related pragmatic resources for developers and managers, please visit us on the web at:

    `http://www.pragmaticprogrammer.com`

Thanks, and remember to make it fun!

---

[1]Expected to be published in 2004.

Preface

Welcome to the world of developer-centric unit testing! We hope you find this book to be a valuable resource for yourself and your project team. You can tell us how it helped you— or let us know how we can improve—by visiting the *Pragmatic Unit Testing* page on our web site[2] and clicking on "Feedback."

Feedback like that is what makes books great. It's also what makes people and projects great. Pragmatic programming is all about using real-world feedback to fine tune and adjust your approach.

Which brings us to unit testing. As we'll see, unit testing is important to you as a programmer because it provides the feedback you need. Without unit testing, you may as well be writing programs on a yellow legal pad and hoping for the best when they're run.

That's not very pragmatic.

This book can help. It is aimed primarily at the C# programmer who has some experience writing and designing code, but who does not have much experience with unit testing.

But while the examples are in C#, using the NUnit framework, the concepts remain the same whether you are writing in C++, Fortran, Ruby, Smalltalk, or VisualBasic. Testing frameworks similar to NUnit exist for over 60 different languages; these various frameworks can be downloaded for free.[3]

---

[2]http://www.pragmaticprogrammer.com/sk/ut/
[3]http://www.xprogramming.com/software.htm

For the more advanced programmer, who has done unit testing before, we hope there will be a couple of nice surprises for you here. Skim over the basics of using NUnit and concentrate on how to think about tests, how testing affects design, and how to handle certain team-wide issues you may be having.

And remember that this book is just the beginning. It may be your first book on unit testing, but we hope it won't be your last.

Where To Find The Code

Throughout the book you'll find examples of C# code; some of these are complete programs while others are fragments of programs. If you want to run any of the example code or look at the complete source (instead of just the printed fragment), look in the margin: the filename of each code fragment in the book is printed in the margin next to the code fragment itself.

Some code fragments evolve with the discussion, so you may find the same source code file (with the same name) in the main directory as well as in subdirectories that contain later versions (rev1, rev2, and so on).

All of the code in this book is available via the *Pragmatic Unit Testing* page on our web site.

Typographic Conventions

italic font   Indicates terms that are being defined, or borrowed from another language.

`computer font`   Indicates method names, file and class names, and various other literal strings.

`xxx xx xx;`   Indicates unimportant portions of source code that are deliberately omitted.

   The "curves ahead" sign warns that this material is more advanced, and can safely be skipped on your first reading.

"Joe the Developer," our cartoon friend, asks a related question that you may find useful.

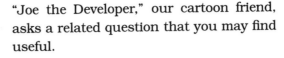 A break in the text where you should stop and think about what's been asked, or try an experiment live on a computer before continuing.

Language-specific Versions

As of this printing, *Pragmatic Unit Testing* is available in two programming language-specific versions:

- in Java with JUnit

- in C# with NUnit

Acknowledgments

We'd especially like to thank the following Practitioners for their valuable input, suggestions, and stories: Mitch Amiano, Nascif Abousalh-Neto, Andrew C. Oliver, Jared Richardson, and Bobby Woolf.

Thanks also to our reviewers who took the time and energy to point out our errors, omissions, and occasionally-twisted writing: Gareth Hayter, Dominique Plante, Charlie Poole, Maik Schmidt, and David Starnes.

Thanks to all of you for your hard work and support.

Andy Hunt and *Dave Thomas*
March, 2004
pragprog@pragmaticprogrammer.com

Chapter 1

Introduction

There are lots of different kinds of testing that can and should be performed on a software project. Some of this testing requires extensive involvement from the end users; other forms may require teams of dedicated Quality Assurance personnel or other expensive resources.

But that's not what we're going to talk about here.

Instead, we're talking about *unit testing*: an essential, if often misunderstood, part of project and personal success. Unit testing is a relatively inexpensive, easy way to produce better code, faster.

Many organizations have grand intentions when it comes to testing, but tend to test only toward the end of a project, when the mounting schedule pressures cause testing to be curtailed or eliminated entirely.

Many programmers feel that testing is just a nuisance: an unwanted bother that merely distracts from the real business at hand—cutting code.

Everyone agrees that more testing is needed, in the same way that everyone agrees you should eat your broccoli, stop smoking, get plenty of rest, and exercise regularly. That doesn't mean that any of us actually do these things, however.

But unit testing can be much more than these—while you might consider it to be in the broccoli family, we're here to tell you that it's more like an awesome sauce that makes everything taste better. Unit testing isn't designed to achieve some corporate quality initiative; it's not a tool for the end-users, or managers, or team leads. Unit testing is done by programmers, for programmers. It's here for our benefit alone, to make our lives easier.

Put simply, unit testing alone can mean the difference between your success and your failure. Consider the following short story.

1.1 Coding With Confidence

Once upon a time—maybe it was last Tuesday—there were two developers, Pat and Dale. They were both up against the same deadline, which was rapidly approaching. Pat was pumping out code pretty fast; developing class after class and method after method, stopping every so often to make sure that the code would compile.

Pat kept up this pace right until the night before the deadline, when it would be time to demonstrate all this code. Pat ran the top-level program, but didn't get any output at all. Nothing. Time to step through using the debugger. Hmm. That can't be right, thought Pat. There's no *way* that this variable could be zero by now. So Pat stepped back through the code, trying to track down the history of this elusive problem.

It was getting late now. That bug was found and fixed, but Pat found several more during the process. And still, there was no output at all. Pat couldn't understand why. It just didn't make any sense.

Dale, meanwhile, wasn't churning out code nearly as fast. Dale would write a new routine and a short test to go along with it. Nothing fancy, just a simple test to see if the routine just written actually did what it was supposed to do. It took a little longer to think of the test, and write it, but Dale refused to move on until the new routine could prove itself. Only then would Dale move up and write the next routine that called it, and so on.

Dale rarely used the debugger, if ever, and was somewhat puzzled at the picture of Pat, head in hands, muttering various evil-sounding curses at the computer with wide, bloodshot eyes staring at all those debugger windows.

The deadline came and went, and Pat didn't make it. Dale's code was integrated and ran almost perfectly. One little glitch came up, but it was pretty easy to see where the problem was. Dale fixed it in just a few minutes.

Now comes the punch line: Dale and Pat are the same age, and have roughly the same coding skills and mental prowess. The only difference is that Dale believes very strongly in unit testing, and tests every newly-crafted method before relying on it or using it from other code.

Pat does not. Pat "knows" that the code should work as written, and doesn't bother to try it until most of the code has been written. But by then it's too late, and it becomes very hard to try to locate the source of bugs, or even determine what's working and what's not.

1.2   What is Unit Testing?

A *unit test* is a piece of code written by a developer that exercises a very small, specific area of functionality of the code being tested. Usually a unit test exercises some particular method in a particular context. For example, you might add a large value to a sorted list, then confirm that this value appears at the end of the list. Or you might delete a pattern of characters from a string and then confirm that they are gone.

Unit tests are performed to prove that a piece of code does what the developer thinks it should do.

The question remains open as to whether that's the right thing to do according to the customer or end-user: that's what acceptance testing is for. We're not really concerned with formal validation and verification or correctness just yet. We're really not even interested in performance testing at this point. All we want to do is prove that code does what we intended, and so we want to test very small, very isolated pieces of functionality. By building up confidence that the individual pieces work as expected, we can then proceed to assemble and test working systems.

After all, if we aren't sure the code is doing what we think, then any other forms of testing may just be a waste of time. You still need other forms of testing, and perhaps much more formal testing depending on your environment. But testing, as with charity, begins at home.

1.3 Why Should I Bother with Unit Testing?

Unit testing will make your life easier. It will make your designs better and drastically reduce the amount of time you spend debugging.

In our tale above, Pat got into trouble by assuming that lower-level code worked, and then went on to use that in higher-level code, which was in turn used by more code, and so on. Without legitimate confidence in any of the code, Pat was building a "house of cards" of assumptions—one little nudge at the bottom and the whole thing falls down.

When basic, low-level code isn't reliable, the requisite fixes don't stay at the low level. You fix the low level problem, but that impacts code at higher levels, which then need fixing, and so on. Fixes begin to ripple throughout the code, getting larger and more complicated as they go. The house of cards falls down, taking the project with it.

Pat keeps saying things like "that's impossible" or "I don't understand how that could happen." If you find yourself thinking these sorts of thoughts, then that's usually a good indication that you don't have enough confidence in your code—you don't know for sure what's working and what's not.

In order to gain the kind of code confidence that Dale has, you'll need to ask the code itself what it is doing, and check that the result is what you expect it to be.

That simple idea describes the heart of unit testing: the single most effective technique to better coding.

1.4 What Do I Want to Accomplish?

It's easy to get carried away with unit testing because it's so much fun, but at the end of the day we still need to produce production code for customers and end-users, so let's be clear about our goals for unit testing. First and foremost, you want to do this to make your life—and the lives of your teammates—easier.

Does It Do What I Want?

Fundamentally, you want to answer the question: "Is the code fulfilling my intent?" The code might well be doing the wrong thing as far as the requirements are concerned, but that's a separate exercise. You want the code to prove to you that it's doing exactly what **you** think it should.

Does It Do What I Want All of the Time?

Many developers who claim they do testing only ever write one test. That's the test that goes right down the middle, taking the "one right path" through the code where everything goes perfectly.

But of course, life is rarely that cooperative, and things don't always go perfectly: exceptions get thrown, disks get full, network lines drop, buffers overflow, and—heaven forbid—we write bugs. That's the "engineering" part of software development. Civil engineers must consider the load on bridges, the effects of high winds, of earthquakes, floods, and so on. Electrical engineers plan on frequency drift, voltage spikes, noise, even problems with parts availability.

You don't test a bridge by driving a single car over it right down the middle lane on a clear, calm day. That's not sufficient. Similarly, beyond ensuring that the code does what you want, you need to ensure that the code does what you want *all of the time*, even when the winds are high, the parameters are suspect, the disk is full, and the network is sluggish.

Can I Depend On It?

Code that you can't depend on is useless. Worse, code that you *think* you can depend on (but turns out to have bugs) can cost you a lot of time to track down and debug. There are very few projects that can afford to waste time, so you want to avoid that "one step forward two steps back" approach at all costs, and stick to moving forward.

No one writes perfect code, and that's okay—as long as you know where the problems exist. Many of the most spectacular software failures that strand broken spacecraft on distant planets or blow them up in mid-flight could have been avoided simply by knowing the limitations of the software. For instance, the Arianne 5 rocket software re-used a library from an older rocket that simply couldn't handle the larger numbers of the higher-flying new rocket.[1] It exploded 40 seconds into flight, taking $500 million dollars with it into oblivion.

We want to be able to depend on the code we write, and know for certain both its strengths and its limitations.

For example, suppose you've written a routine to reverse a list of numbers. As part of testing, you give it an empty list— and the code blows up. The requirements don't say you have to accept an empty list, so maybe you simply document that fact in the comment block for the method and throw an exception if the routine is called with an empty list. Now you know the limitations of code right away, instead of finding out the hard way (often somewhere inconvenient, such as in the upper atmosphere).

Does it Document my Intent?

One nice side-effect of unit testing is that it helps you communicate the code's intended use. In effect, a unit test behaves as executable documentation, showing how you expect the code to behave under the various conditions you've considered.

---

[1] For aviation geeks: The numeric overflow was due to a much larger "horizontal bias" due to a different trajectory that increased the horizontal velocity of the rocket.

Team members can look at the tests for examples of how to use your code. If someone comes across a test case that you haven't considered, they'll be alerted quickly to that fact.

And of course, executable documentation has the benefit of being correct. Unlike written documentation, it won't drift away from the code (unless, of course, you stop running the tests).

1.5 How Do I Do Unit Testing?

Unit testing is basically an easy practice to adopt, but there are some guidelines and common steps that you can follow to make it easier and more effective.

The first step is to decide how to test the method in question—before writing the code itself. With at least a rough idea of how to proceed, you proceed to write the test code itself, either before or concurrently with the implementation code.

Next, you run the test itself, and probably all the other tests in that part of the system, or even the entire system's tests if that can be done relatively quickly. It's important that **all the tests pass**, not just the new one. You want to avoid any collateral damage as well as any immediate bugs.

Every test needs to determine whether it passed or not—it doesn't count if you or some other hapless human has to read through a pile of output and decide whether the code worked or not. You want to get into the habit of looking at the test results and telling at a glance whether it all worked. We'll talk more about that when we go over the specifics of using unit testing frameworks.

1.6 Excuses For Not Testing

Despite our rational and impassioned pleas, some developers will still nod their heads and agree with the need for unit testing, but will steadfastly assure us that *they* couldn't possibly do this sort of testing for one of a variety of reasons. Here are some of the most popular excuses we've heard, along with our rebuttals.

> ∖∕⁄ **Joe Asks...**
>
> **What's collateral damage?**
>
> *Collateral damage* is what happens when a new fea-
> ture or a bug fix in one part of the system causes a
> bug (damage) to another, possibly unrelated part of
> the system. It's an insidious problem that, if allowed to
> continue, can quickly render the entire system broken
> beyond anyone's ability to fix.
>
> We sometime call this the "Whac-a-Mole" effect. In
> the carnival game of Whac-a-Mole, the player must
> strike the mechanical mole heads that pop up on the
> playing field. But they don't keep their heads up for
> long; as soon as you move to strike one mole, it re-
> treats and another mole pops up on the opposite side
> of the field. The moles pop up and down fast enough
> that it can be very frustrating to try to connect with
> one and score. As a result, players generally flail help-
> lessly at the field as the moles continue to pop up
> where you least expect them.
>
> Widespread collateral damage to a code base can
> have a similar effect.

It takes too much time to write the tests This is the number one complaint voiced by most newcomers to unit testing.
It's untrue, of course, but to see why we need to take a closer
look at where you spend your time when developing code.

Many people view testing of any sort as something that happens toward the end of a project. And yes, if you wait to begin
unit testing until then it will definitely take too long. In fact,
you may not finish the job until the heat death of the universe
itself.

At least it will feel that way: it's like trying to clear a couple of
acres of land with a lawn mower. If you start early on when
there's just a field of grasses, the job is easy. If you wait
until later, when the field contains thick, gnarled trees and
dense, tangled undergrowth, then the job becomes impossibly
difficult.

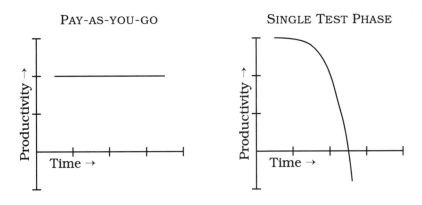

Figure 1.1: COMPARISON OF PAYING-AS-YOU-GO VS. HAVING A SINGLE TESTING PHASE

Instead of waiting until the end, it's far cheaper in the long run to adopt the "pay-as-you-go" model. By writing individual tests with the code itself as you go along, there's no crunch at the end, and you experience fewer overall bugs as you are generally always working with tested code. By taking a little extra time all the time, you minimize the risk of needing a huge amount of time at the end.

You see, the trade-off is not "test now" versus "test later." It's linear work now versus exponential work and complexity trying to fix and rework at the end: not only is the job larger and more complex, but now you have to re-learn the code you wrote some weeks or months ago. All that extra work kills your productivity, as shown in Figure 1.1.

Notice that testing isn't free. In the pay-as-you-go model, the effort is not zero; it will cost you some amount of effort (and time and money). But look at the frightening direction the right-hand curve takes over time—straight down. Your productivity might even become negative. These productivity losses can easily doom a project.

So if you think you don't have time to write tests in addition to the code you're already writing, consider the following questions:

1. How much time do you spend debugging code that you or others have written?

2. How much time do you spend reworking code that you thought was working, but turned out to have major, crippling bugs?

3. How much time do you spend isolating a reported bug to its source?

For most people who work without unit tests, these numbers add up fast, and will continue to add up even faster over the life of the project. Proper unit testing dramatically reduces these times, which frees up enough time so that you'll have the opportunity to write all of the unit tests you want—and maybe even some free time to spare.

It takes too long to run the tests It shouldn't. Most unit tests should execute extremely quickly, so you should be able to run hundreds, even thousands of them in a matter of a few seconds. But sometimes that won't be possible, and you may end up with certain tests that simply take too long to conveniently run all of the time.

In that case, you'll want to separate out the longer-running tests from the short ones. Only run the long tests once a day, or once every few days as appropriate, and run the shorter tests constantly.

It's not my job to test my code Now here's an interesting excuse. Pray tell, what *is* your job, exactly? Presumably your job, at least in part, is to create working code. If you are throwing code over the wall to some testing group without any assurance that it's working, then you're not doing your job. It's not polite to expect others to clean up our own messes, and in extreme cases submitting large volumes of buggy code can become a "career limiting" move.

On the other hand, if the testers or QA group find it very difficult to find fault with your code, your reputation will grow rapidly—along with your job security!

I don't really know how the code is supposed to behave so I can't test it If you truly don't know how the code is supposed to behave, then maybe this isn't the time to be writing it. Maybe a prototype would be more appropriate as a first step to help clarify the requirements.

If you don't know what the code is supposed to do, then how will you know that it does it?

But it compiles! Okay, no one *really* comes out with this as an excuse, at least not out loud. But it's easy to get lulled into thinking that a successful compile is somehow a mark of approval, that you've passed some threshold of goodness.

But the compiler's blessing is a pretty shallow compliment. It can verify that your syntax is correct, but it can't figure out what your code should do. For example, the C# compiler can easily determine that this line is wrong:

```
statuc void Main() {
```

It's just a simple typo, and should be static, not statuc. That's the easy part. But now suppose you've written the following:

```
public void Addit(Object anObject) {
  List myList = new List();
  myList.Add(anObject);
  myList.Add(anObject);
  // more code...
}
```

Main.cs

Did you really mean to add the same object to the same list twice? Maybe, maybe not. The compiler can't tell the difference, only you know what you've intended the code to do.[2]

I'm being paid to write code, not to write tests By that same logic, you're not being paid to spend all day in the debugger, either. Presumably you are being paid to write *working* code, and unit tests are merely a tool toward that end, in the same fashion as an editor, an IDE, or the compiler.

---

[2]Automated testing tools that generate their own tests based on your existing code fall into this same trap—they can only use what you wrote, not what you meant.

I feel guilty about putting testers and QA staff out of work
Not to worry, you won't. Remember we're only talking about
unit testing, here. It's the barest-bones, lowest-level testing
that's designed for us, the programmers. There's plenty of
other work to be done in the way of functional testing, acceptance testing, performance and environmental testing, validation and verification, formal analysis, and so on.

**My company won't let me run unit tests on the live sys-
tem** Whoa! We're talking about developer unit-testing here.
While you might be able to run those same tests in other con-
texts (on the live, production system, for instance) *they are no
longer unit tests.* Run your unit tests on your machine, using
your own database, or using a mock object (see Chapter 6).

If the QA department or other testing staff want to run these
tests in a production or staging environment, you might be
able to coordinate the technical details with them so they can,
but realize that they are no longer unit tests in that context.

1.7 Roadmap

Chapter 2, *Your First Unit Tests*, contains an overview of test
writing. From there we'll take a look at the specifics of *Writing
Tests in NUnit* in Chapter 3. We'll then spend a few chapters
on how you come up with *what* things need testing, and how
to test them.

Next we'll look at the important properties of good tests in
Chapter 7. We then talk about what you need to do to use
testing effectively in your project in Chapter 8. This chapter also discusses how to handle existing projects with lots
of legacy code. Chapter 9, *Design Issues.* then looks at how
testing can influence your application's design (for the better).

The appendices contain additional useful information: a look
at common unit testing problems, a note on installing NUnit,
and a list of resources including the bibliography. We finish
off with a summary card containing highlights of the book's
tips and suggestions.

So sit back, relax, and welcome to the world of better coding.

Chapter 2

Your First Unit Tests

As we said in the introduction, a unit test is just a piece of code. It's a piece of code you write that happens to exercise another piece of code, and determines whether the other piece of code is behaving as expected or not.

How do you do that, exactly?

To check if code is behaving as you expect, you use an *assertion*, a simple method call that verifies that something is true. For instance, the method IsTrue checks that the given boolean condition is true, and fails the current test if it is not. It might be implemented like the following.

```
public void IsTrue(bool condition) {
  if (!condition) {
    abort();
  }
}
```

You could use this assert to check all sorts of things, including whether numbers are equal to each other:

```
int a = 2;
... ... .. . ... .;
. . . .. ... ... ..
IsTrue(a == 2);
.... .. .. ... ..;
```

If for some reason a does not equal 2 when the method IsTrue is called, then the program will abort.

Since we check for equality a lot, it might be easier to have an assert just for numbers. To check that two integers are equal,

AssertTrue.cs

for instance, we could write a method that takes two integer parameters:

```
public void AreEqual(int a, int b) {
  IsTrue(a == b);
}
```

Armed with just these two asserts, we can start writing some tests. We'll look at more asserts and describe the details of how you use asserts in unit test code in the next chapter. But first, let's consider what tests might be needed before we write any code at all.

2.1 Planning Tests

We'll start with a simple example, a single, static method designed to find the largest number in a list of numbers:

```
static int Largest(int[] list);
```

In other words, given an array of numbers such as [7, 8, 9], this method should return 9. That's a reasonable first test. What other tests can you think of, off the top of your head? Take a minute and write down as many tests as you can think of for this simple method before you continue reading.

Think about this for a moment before reading on. . .

How many tests did you come up with?

It shouldn't matter what order the given list is in, so right off the bat you've got the following test ideas (which we've written as "what you pass in" → "what you expect").

- [7, 8, 9] → 9

- [8, 9, 7] → 9

- [9, 7, 8] → 9

What happens if there are duplicate largest numbers?

- [7, 9, 8, 9] → 9

Since these are `int` types, not objects, you probably don't care which 9 is returned, as long as one of them is.

What if there's only one number?

- `[1] → 1`

And what happens with negative numbers:

- `[-9, -8, -7] → -7`

It might look odd, but indeed -7 is larger than -9. Glad we straightened that out now, rather than in the debugger or in production code where it might not be so obvious.

To make all this more concrete, lets actually write a "largest" method and test it. Here's the code for our first implementation:

```
Line 1  public class Cmp {

            ///
            /// <summary>
    5       /// Return the largest element in a list.
            /// </summary>
            /// <param name="list"> A list of integers </param>
            /// <returns>
            /// The largest number in the given list
   10       /// </returns>
            ///
            public static int Largest(int[] list) {
              int index, max=Int32.MaxValue;
              for (index = 0; index < list.Length-1; index++) {
   15           if (list[index] > max) {
                  max = list[index];
                }
              }
              return max;
   20       }

          }
```

Largest.cs

Now that we've got some ideas for tests, we'll look at writing these tests in C#, using the NUnit framework.

2.2 Testing a Simple Method

Normally you want to make the first test you write incredibly simple, because there is much to be tested the first time besides the code itself: all of that messy business of class names, assembly references, and making sure it compiles. You want to get all of that taken care of and out of the way with the very first, simplest test; you won't have to worry about it anymore after that, and you won't have to debug complex integration issues at the same time you're debugging a complex test!

First, let's just test the simple case of passing in a small array with a couple of unique numbers. Here's the complete source code for the test class. We'll explain all about test classes in the next chapter; for now, just concentrate on the assert statements:

```
using NUnit.Framework;
[TestFixture]
public class TestLargest {
  [Test]
  public void LargestOf3() {
    Assert.AreEqual(9, Cmp.Largest(new int[] {8,9,7}));
  }
}
```

C# note: the odd-looking syntax to create an anonymous array is just for your authors' benefit, as we are lazy and do not like to type. If you prefer, the test could be written this way instead (although the previous syntax is idiomatic):

```
[Test]
public void LargestOf3Alt() {
  int[] arr = new int[3];
  arr[0] = 8;
  arr[1] = 9;
  arr[2] = 7;
  Assert.AreEqual(9, Cmp.Largest(arr));
}
```

That's all it takes, and you have your first test.

We want to run this simple test and make sure it passes; to do that, we need to take a quick look at running tests using NUnit.

2.3 Running Tests with NUnit

NUnit is a freely available,[1] open source product that provides a testing framework and test runners. It's available as C# source code that you can compile and install yourself, and also as a Microsoft Installer (MSI) file.

---

[1]http://www.nunit.org

Joe Asks...

What's the deal with Open Source?

What is open source, exactly? *Open source* refers to software where the source code is made freely available. Typically this means that you can obtain the product for free, and that you are also free to modify it, add to it, give it to your friends, and so on.

Is it safe to use? For the most part, open source products are safer to use than their commercial, closed-source counterparts, because they are open to examination by thousands of other interested developers. Malicious programs, spyware, viruses, and other similar problems are rare to non-existent in the open source community.

Is it legal? Absolutely. Just as you are free to write a song or a book and give it away (or sell it), you are free to write code and give it away (or sell it). There are a variety of open source licenses that clarify the freedoms involved. Before you distribute any code that includes open source components, you should carefully check the particular license agreements involved.

Can I contribute? We certainly hope so! The strength of open source comes from people all over the world: People just like you, who know how to program and have a need for some particular feature. Would you like to add a feature to NUnit? You can! You can edit the source code to the library or one of the test runners and change it, and use those changes yourself. You can e-mail your changes to the maintainers of the product, and they may even incorporate your changes into the next release.

The easiest way to install NUnit is to run the MSI file, which will launch a familiar Windows Installer wizard. Note that MSI support is built in to Windows 2000 and XP; for Windows 95, 98, ME and NT4.0, you'll need to download the installer service from Microsoft's web site for your particular operating system (search for "Windows Installer Redistributable" on www.microsoft.com). Linux fans may want to look at Mono, an open-source port of .NET for the Linux environment. It ships with its own version of NUnit.

Next, you need to compile the code we've shown. If you're using Visual Studio, create a new project for this sample code of type *Class Library*. Type our "production" code into a file named Largest.cs, and our new test code into a file named TestLargest.cs. If you'd rather not type these programs in from scratch, you'll be pleased to know that all of the source code for this book is available from our website.[2])

Notice that the test code uses NUnit.Framework; you'll need to add a reference to nunit.framework.dll in order to compile this code. In Visual Studio, select "Project" from the main menu and then select "Add Reference...". Once there, select "nunit.framework" from the .NET tab, and press the SELECT button to add the dll to the component list as shown in Figure 2.1. Press OK, and now your project will be able to use the functionality of the NUnit framework.

Go ahead and build the project as you normally would (In Visual Studio, CTRL-SHIFT-B works well). Now you've got an assembly. But it's just a library. How can we run it?

Test Runners to the rescue! A test runner knows to look for the [TestFixture] attribute of a class, and for the [Test] methods within it. The runner will run the tests, accumulate some statistics on which tests passed and failed, and report the results back to you.

There are three main ways to use a test runner:

1. NUnit GUI
2. NUnit command line
3. Add-in to Visual Studio

---

[2]http://www.pragmaticprogrammer.com/sk/ut/

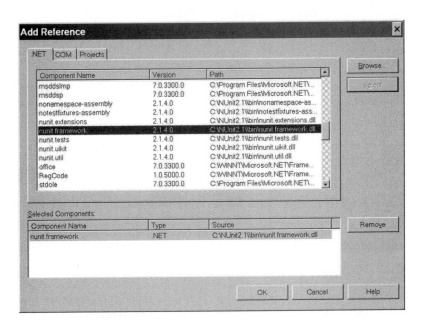

Figure 2.1: ADDING NUNIT ASSEMBLY REFERENCE

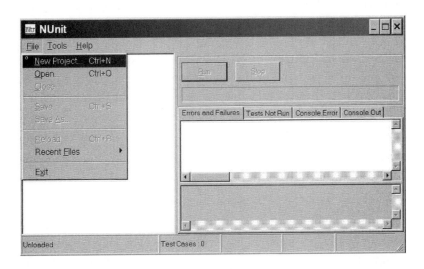

Figure 2.2: CREATING A NEW NUNIT PROJECT

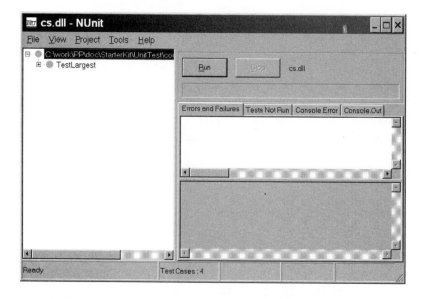

Figure 2.3: NUNIT LOADED AND READY

NUnit GUI

The NUnit GUI can be started from the desktop icon or from the Windows Start menu. When the GUI comes up, you've got a couple of choices. You can create a new NUnit project as shown in Figure 2.2 on the page before; navigate to your source directory and create the NUnit project file. Then under the "Project" menu, add assemblies or Visual Studio projects to your NUnit project.[3]

Alternatively, you can just Open an assembly (a .dll file) directly. In Figure 2.3, we've loaded our test directly from the dll. It's ready to be tested by pressing the "Run" button.

When you run a selected test, the GUI will display a large, colored, status bar. If all the tests pass, the bar is a happy shade of bright green. If any test fails, the bar becomes an angry red. If the bar is a cautionary yellow, that means some tests were skipped (more on that later).

---

[3]Visual Studio support can be enabled using a preference located under Tools/Options.

Figure 2.4: ADDING TO THE WINDOWS SYSTEM PATH

NUnit Command Line

NUnit can also be run from the command line, which comes in very handy when automating the project build and test. You'll need to add the NUnit `bin` directory to your path (that is, the directory path to wherever you installed the NUnit application, plus "\bin").

For the current shell, you can set your path variable at the command line, as in the following example.

```
C:\> set "PATH=%PATH%;C:\Program Files\Nunit V2.2\bin"
```

For more permanent use, go to Control Panel/System/Advanced/Environment Variable and add NUnit's `bin` directory to the `Path` variable (see Figure 2.4).

```
C:\> nunit-console cs.dll
NUnit version 2.1.4
Copyright (C) 2002-2003 James W. Newkirk, Michael C. Two, Alexei A. Vorontsov,
Charlie Poole.
Copyright (C) 2000-2003 Philip Craig.
All Rights Reserved.

....
Tests run: 4, Failures: 0, Not run: 0, Time: 0.046875 seconds

C:\> _
```

Figure 2.5: NUNIT COMMAND LINE USAGE

To run from the command line, type the command nunit-console followed by an NUnit project file or a dll. You'll see output something like that shown in Figure 2.5.

NUnit Add-in to Visual Studio

Finally, there are several add-ins that integrate NUnit with Visual Studio.[4] nunit-addin adds the ability to run any test just by right-clicking on the source code and selecting "Run Test(s)"; the output from the tests are reported in Visual Studio's output pane. Other similar projects add visual reporting of tests and other features.

2.4 Running the Example

You should be ready to run this first test now.

Try running this example before reading on...

---

[4]Such as http://www.mutantdesign.co.uk/nunit-addin/

Having just run that code, you probably saw an error similar to the following:

```
Failures:
1) TestLargest.LargestOf3 :
        expected:<9>
          but was:<2147483647>
   at TestLargest.LargestOf3() in c:\testlargest.cs:line 6
```

Whoops! That didn't go as expected. Why did it return such a huge number instead of our 9? Where could that very large number have come from? It almost looks like the largest number... oh, it's a small typo: `max=Int32.MaxValue` on line 13 should have been `max=0`. We want to initialize max so that any other number instantly becomes the next max. Let's fix the code, recompile, and run the test again to make sure that it works.

Next we'll look at what happens when the largest number appears in different places in the list—first or last, and somewhere in the middle. Bugs most often show up at the "edges." In this case, edges occur when when the largest number is at the start or end of the array that we pass in. We can lump all three of these asserts together in one test, but let's add the assert statements one at a time. We already have the case with the largest in the middle:

```
using NUnit.Framework;
[TestFixture]
public class TestLargest {

  [Test]
  public void LargestOf3() {
    Assert.AreEqual(9, Cmp.Largest(new int[] {8,9,7}));
  }
}
```

TestLargest.cs

Now try it with the 9 as the first value (we'll just add an additional assertion to the existing `LargestOf3()` method):

```
  [Test]
  public void LargestOf3() {
    Assert.AreEqual(9, Cmp.Largest(new int[] {9,8,7}));
    Assert.AreEqual(9, Cmp.Largest(new int[] {8,9,7}));
  }
```

TestLargest.cs

We're on a roll. One more, just for the sake of completeness, and we can move on to more interesting tests:

```
[Test]
public void LargestOf3() {
  Assert.AreEqual(9, Cmp.Largest(new int[] {9,8,7}));
  Assert.AreEqual(9, Cmp.Largest(new int[] {8,9,7}));
  Assert.AreEqual(9, Cmp.Largest(new int[] {7,8,9}));
}
```

Try running this example before reading on. . .

```
Failures:
1) TestLargest.LargestOf3 :
        expected:<9>
          but was:<8>
    at TestLargest.LargestOf3() in c:\testlargest.cs:line 5
```

Why did the test get an 8 as the largest number? It's almost as if the code ignored the last entry in the list. Sure enough, another simple typo: the `for` loop is terminating too early. This is an example of the infamous "off-by-one" error. Our code has:

```
for (index = 0; index < list.Length-1; index++) {
```

But it should be one of:

```
for (index = 0; index <= list.Length-1; index++) {
for (index = 0; index < list.Length; index++) {
```

The second expression is idiomatic in languages descended from C (including Java and C#), but as you can see, it's prone to off-by-one errors. Make the changes and run the tests again, but consider that this sort of bug is telling you something: it would be better to use an iterator (using the C# `foreach` statement) here instead. That way you could avoid this kind of off-by-one error in the future.

Let's check for duplicate largest values; type this in and run it (we'll only show the newly added methods from here on):

```
[Test]
public void TestDups() {
  Assert.AreEqual(9, Cmp.Largest(new int[] {9,7,9,8}));
}
```

So far, so good. Now the test for just a single integer:

```
[Test]
public void TestOne() {
   Assert.AreEqual(1, Cmp.Largest(new int[] {1}));
}
```

Hey, it worked! You're on a roll now, surely all the bugs we planted in this example have been exorcised by now. Just one more check with negative values:

```
[Test]
public void TestNegative() {
  int [] negList = new int[] {-9, -8, -7};
  Assert.AreEqual(-7, Cmp.Largest(negList));
}
```

TestLargest.cs

Try running this example before reading on. . .

STOP

```
Failures:
1) TestLargest.TestNegative :
        expected:<-7>
        but was:<0>
   at TestLargest.TestNegative() in c:\testlargest.cs:line 4
```

Whoops! Where did zero come from?

Looks like choosing 0 to initialize max was a bad idea; what we really wanted was MinValue, so as to be less than all negative numbers as well:

```
max = Int32.MinValue
```

Make that change and try it again—all of the existing tests should continue to pass, and now this one will as well.

Unfortunately, the initial specification for the method "largest" is incomplete, as it doesn't say what should happen if the array is empty. Let's say that it's an error, and add some code at the top of the method that will throw a runtime-exception if the list length is zero:

```
public static int Largest(int[] list) {
  int index, max=Int32.MinValue;
  if (list.Length == 0) {
    throw new ArgumentException("largest: Empty list");
  }
  // ...
```

Largest.cs

Notice that just by thinking of the tests, we've already realized we need a design change. That's not at all unusual, and in fact is something we want to capitalize on. So for the last test, we need to check that an exception is thrown when passing in an empty array. We'll talk about testing exceptions in depth on page 41, but for now just trust us:

```
[Test, ExpectedException(typeof(ArgumentException))]
public void TestEmpty() {
  Cmp.Largest(new int[] {});
}
```

Finally, a reminder: all code—test or production—should be clear and simple. Test code *especially* must be easy to understand, even at the expense of performance or verbosity.

2.5 More Tests

We started with a very simple method and came up with a couple of interesting tests that actually found some bugs. Note that we didn't go overboard and blindly try every possible number combination; we picked the interesting cases that might expose problems. But are these all the tests you can think of for this method?

What other tests might be appropriate?

Since we'll need to think up tests all of the time, maybe we need a way to think about code that will help us to come up with good tests regularly and reliably. We'll talk about that after the next chapter, but first, let's take a more in-depth look at using NUnit.

Chapter 3

Writing Tests in NUnit

We've looked at writing tests somewhat informally in the last chapter, but now it's time to take a deeper look at the difference between test code and production code, all the various forms of NUnit's assertions, the structure and composition of NUnit tests, and so on.

3.1 Structuring Unit Tests

If you have a method named `CreateAccount` that you want to test, then your first test method might be named something like `CreateSimpleAccount`. The method `CreateSimpleAccount` will call `CreateAccount` with the necessary parameters and verify that `CreateAccount` works as advertised. You can, of course, have many test methods that exercise `CreateAccount` (not all accounts are simple, after all).

The relationship between these two pieces of code is shown in Figure 3.1 on the following page.

The test code is for our internal use only. Customers or end-users will never see it or use it. The production code—that is, the code that will eventually be shipped to a customer and put into production—must therefore not know anything about the test code. Production code will be thrust out into the cold world all alone, without the test code. (This typically means that test code is placed under a different project, in its own assembly).

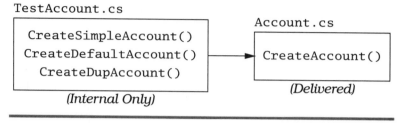

Figure 3.1: TEST CODE AND PRODUCTION CODE

The test code must be written to do a few things:

- Set up all conditions needed for testing (create any required objects, allocate any needed resources, etc.)

- Call the method to be tested

- Verify that the tested method functioned as expected

- Clean up after itself

You write test code and compile it in the normal fashion, as you would any other bit of source code in your project. It might happen to use some additional libraries, but otherwise there's no magic—it's just regular code.

When it's time to execute the code, remember that you never actually run the production code directly; at least, not the way a user would. Instead, you run the test code, which in turn exercises the production code under very carefully controlled conditions.

Now, although you *could* write all your tests from the ground up, that's not terribly efficient. For for the rest of this book we'll assume that you're using the NUnit framework. More specifically, we'll be showing the specific method calls and classes for NUnit 2.2, using C#, in our examples. Earlier or later versions may have slight differences from the details presented here, but the general concepts are the same across all versions, and indeed for any testing framework in any language or environment.

3.2 NUnit Asserts

As we've seen, there are some helper methods that assist you in determining whether a method under test is performing correctly or not. Generically, we call all these methods *assertions*. They let you assert that some condition is true; that two bits of data are equal, or not, and so on. We'll take a look at each one of the assert methods that NUnit provides next.

All of the following methods will record failures (that's when the assertion is false) or errors (that's when you get an unexpected exception), and report these through the NUnit classes. For the text version, that means an error message will be printed to the console. The GUI version will show a red bar and supporting details to indicate a failure.

When a failure or error occurs, execution of the current test method is aborted. Other tests within the same test fixture will still be run.

Asserts are the fundamental building block for unit tests; the NUnit library provides a number of different forms of assert as static methods in the `Assert` class.

AreEqual

```
Assert.AreEqual(expected, actual [, string message])
```

This is the most-often used form of assert. *expected* is a value you hope to see (typically hard-coded), and *actual* is a value actually produced by the code under test. *message* is an optional message that will be reported in the event of a failure. You can omit the message argument and simply provide the *expected* and *actual* values.

Any kind of object may be tested for equality; the appropriate equals method will be used for the comparison. In particular, you can compare the contents of strings using this method. Different method signatures are also provided for all the native types (`int`, `decimal`, etc.) and `Object`.

Computers cannot represent all floating-point numbers exactly, and will usually be off a little bit. Because of this, if you are using an assert to compare floating point numbers (floats or doubles in C#), you need to specify one additional piece of information, the tolerance. This specifies just how close to "equals" you need the result to be.

```
Assert.AreEqual(expected,
                actual,
                tolerance [, string message])
```

For business applications, 4 or 5 decimal places is probably enough. For scientific apps, you may need greater precision.

As an example, the following assert will check that the actual result is equal to 3.33, but only look at the first two decimal places:

```
Assert.AreEqual(3.33, 10.0/3.0, 0.01, "Wanted 3 1/3");
```

IsNull

```
Assert.IsNull(object [, string message])
Assert.IsNotNull(object [, string message])
```

Asserts that the given object is null (or not null), failing otherwise. The message is optional.

AreSame

```
Assert.AreSame(expected, actual [, string message])
```

Asserts that *expected* and *actual* refer to the same object, and fails the test if they do not. The message is optional.

IsTrue

```
Assert.IsTrue(bool condition [, string message])
```

Asserts that the given boolean condition is true, otherwise the test fails. The message is optional.

If you find test code that is littered with the following:

```
Assert.IsTrue(true);
```

then you should rightfully be concerned. Unless that construct is used to verify some sort of branching or exception logic, it's probably a bad idea. In particular, what you really don't want to see is a whole page of "test" code with a single Assert.IsTrue(true) at the very end (i.e., "the code made it to the very end without blowing up therefore it must work"). That's not testing, that's wishful thinking.

In addition to testing for `true`, you can also test for `false`:

```
Assert.IsFalse(bool condition [, string message])
```

Asserts that the given boolean condition is false, otherwise the test fails. The message is optional.

Fail

```
Assert.Fail([string message])
```

Fails the test immediately, with the optional message. This might be used to mark sections of code that should not be reached, but isn't really used much in practice.

Using Asserts

You usually have multiple asserts in a given test method, as you prove various aspects and relationships of the method(s) under test. When an assert fails, that test method will be aborted—the remaining assertions in that method will not be executed this time. But that shouldn't be of any concern; you have to fix the failing test before you can proceed anyway. And you fix the next failing test. And the next. And so on.

You should normally expect that all tests pass all of the time. In practice, that means that when you introduce a bug, only one or two tests fail. Isolating the problem is usually pretty easy in that environment.

Under no circumstances should you continue to add features when there are failing tests! Fix any test as soon as it fails, and keep all tests passing all of the time.

To maintain that discipline, you'll need an easy way to run all the tests—or to run groups of tests, particular subsystems, and so on.

3.3 NUnit Framework

So far, we've just looked at the assert methods themselves. But you can't just stick assert methods into a source file and expect it to work; you need a little bit more of a framework than that. Fortunately, it's not too much more.

Here is a very simple piece of test code that illustrates the minimum framework you need to get started.

```
Line 1   using NUnit.Framework;
   -     [TestFixture]
   -     public class TestSimple {
   -       [Test]
   5       public void LargestOf3() {
   -         Assert.AreEqual(9, Cmp.Largest(new int[] {8,9,7}));
   -       }
   -     }
```

This code is pretty straightforward, but let's take a look at each part in turn.

First, the using statement on line 1 brings in the necessary NUnit classes. The NUnit framework provides the unit-testing functionality that we'll need, including all of the assert methods we described above. (Remember you'll need to add a reference in your project to the NUnit DLL in order for the using statement to work).

Next, we have the class definition itself on line 3: each class that contains tests must be annotated with a [TestFixture] attribute as shown. The class must be declared public (so that the test runners can find it), and it must have a public, no-parameter, constructor (the default constructor is fine).

Finally, the test class contains individual methods annotated with [Test] attributes. In the example, we've got one test method named LargestOf3 on line 5. Any public method specified with a [Test] attribute will be run automatically by NUnit.

In the previous example, we showed a single test, using a single assert, in a single test method. Of course, inside a test method, you can place any number of asserts:

```
using NUnit.Framework;
[TestFixture]
public class TestSimple {
  [Test]
  public void LargestOf3() {
    Assert.AreEqual(9, Cmp.Largest(new int[] {8,9,7}));
    Assert.AreEqual(100, Cmp.Largest(new int[] {100,4,25}));
    Assert.AreEqual(64, Cmp.Largest(new int[] {1,64,38}));
  }
}
```

Here we have three calls to `Assert.AreEqual` inside a test method.

3.4 NUnit Test Selection

As we've seen so far, a fixture (that is, a class marked with the `[TestFixture]` attribute) contains test methods; each method contains one or more assertions. Multiple test fixtures can be included into an assembly.

You will normally run all of the tests within an assembly just by specifying the assembly to the test runner. You can also choose to run individual test fixtures within an assembly using either the NUnit command line or GUI.

From the GUI, you can select an individual test, a single test fixture, or the entire assembly by clicking on it, and all the appropriate tests will be run.

From the command line, you can specify the assembly and a particular test fixture as follows:

```
c:\> nunit-console assemblyname.dll /fixture:ClassName
```

Given this flexibility, you may want to think a bit about how to organize test methods into individual assemblies and fixtures to make testing easier.

For instance, you may want to run all the database-related tests at once, or all of the tests that Fred wrote (Fred is still on probation from the last project, and you want to keep an eye on him).

But suppose you have the database-related tests in one fixture, and Fred's tests in another fixture, and you'd like to run both of these fixtures together. It's a bit of a pain to have to manually select both fixtures each time (whether you're using the command line or the GUI), and you don't want Fred to write all of his tests in your database fixture.

Fortunately, you can combine existing test fixtures into a *test suite*. A test suite is a collection of `TextFixture` classes. Any test class can contain a static method that is marked with the attribute `[Suite]`. This method returns a `TestSuite`, which is a collection of `TestFixture` classes.

```
using NUnit.Framework;
using NUnit.Core; // Requires nunit.core.dll
[TestFixture]
public class TestClassSuite {
  [Suite]
  public static TestSuite Suite {
    get {
      TestSuite suite = new TestSuite("Name of Suite");
      suite.Add(new DatabaseTests());
      suite.Add(new FredsTests());
      // add others...
      return suite;
    }
  }
}
```

The classes you add to the suite (DatabaseTests, Freds-
Tests and so on) are marked as [TestFixture] classes.
Within each of these classes you still have the [Test] attribute on individual methods, and the framework will run
those automatically. The suite facility doesn't stop you running the individual fixtures when you want. But they also let
you group those fixtures: by running the one Suite(), you
can now run a whole bunch of test fixtures at once.

Suites are a useful mechanism for composing tests hierar-
chically, which can be handy for coordinating sets of tests
especially for an unattended build.

But it's not that useful a mechanism for day-to-day testing.
You'd like to be able to cross-cut across all the tests and select
or exclude certain kinds of tests from the vast pool of existing
tests you've written.

Fortunately, NUnit has another mechanism you can use to
categorize and classify individual test methods and fixtures.

Categories

NUnit provides an easy way to mark and run individual tests
and fixtures by using *categories*. A category is just a name
that you define. You can associate different test methods with
one or more categories, and then select which categories you
want to run when running the tests.

Suppose among your tests you've got a method to find the
shortest route that our traveling salesman, Bob, can take to

visit the top n cities in his territory. The funny thing about the Traveling Salesman algorithm is that for a small number of cities it works just fine, but it's an *exponential* algorithm. That means that a few hundred cities might take 20,000 years to run, for example. Even 50 cities takes a few hours, so you probably don't want to to include that test by default.

You can use NUnit categories to help sort out short tests that you can run constantly versus long-running tests that you'd rather only run during the nightly build.

A category is specified as an attribute. You provide a string to identify the category when you declare the method. Then when you run the tests, you can specify which categories you want to run (you can specify more than one).

For instance, suppose you've got a few methods that only take a few seconds to run, but one method that takes a long time to run. You can annotate them using the category names "Short" and "Long" (you might also consider making a category "Fred" if you still want to keep an eye on him.)

```
Line 1    using NUnit.Framework;
    -     using NUnit.Core;
    -
    -     [TestFixture]
    5     public class TestShortestPath {
    -
    -       [Test]
    -       [Category("Short")]
    -       public void Use5Cities() {
   10         TSP tsp = new TSP(); // Load with default cities
    -          Assert.AreEqual(140, tsp.ShortestPath(5));
    -       }
    -
    -       [Test, Category("Short")] // Can specify either way
   15       public void Use10Cities() {
    -          TSP tsp = new TSP(); // Load with default cities
    -          Assert.AreEqual(586, tsp.ShortestPath(10));
    -       }
    -
   20       // This one takes a while...
    -       [Test]
    -       [Category("Long")]
    -       public void Use50Cities() {
    -          TSP tsp = new TSP(); // Load with default cities
   25         Assert.AreEqual(2300, tsp.ShortestPath(50));
    -       }
    -     }
```

TestShortestPath.cs

Notice that you can specify multiple attributes (in this case, `Test` and `Category`) on two separate lines as shown around

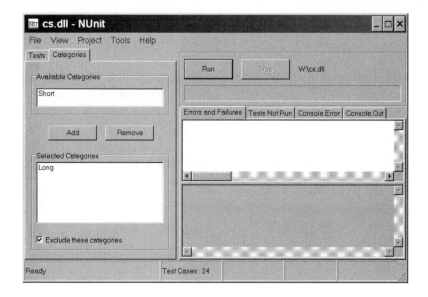

Figure 3.2: NUNIT CATEGORY SELECTION

line 8, or combined into one line as shown on line 14.

Now if you choose to run just "Short" methods, the two methods Use2Cities and Use10Cities will be selected to run. If you choose "Long" methods, only Use50Cities will be selected. You can also select both categories to run all three of these methods.

In the GUI, you select which categories to run on the tab as shown in Figure 3.2 on the current page. Just select each category you're interested and press the ADD button.

From the command line, you can specify individual categories to include as well. Just add the following parameter to the command line:

```
/include=string;string,...
```

Note that multiple category names are separated by a semi-colon (";").

You can also choose to *exclude* the listed categories so all other tests except those in the named categories run. There's a check box in the GUI for this; the command line option is, oddly enough, /exclude.

But this isn't quite enough: it turns out that some categories of tests should be run when no categories are selected, while others should run only when explicitly selected.

To support this, you can specify the Explicit property to the [Category] attribute:

```
[Category("SpecialEquipmentNeeded", Explicit=true)]
```

This syntax automatically excludes the category from a run that doesn't specify any categories. By default, your run will include tests without categories and tests with non-explicit categories. However, if even one category is specified in the GUI or the command line, then only that single category will be run.

In addition to marking individual test methods as belonging to a category, you can also mark entire fixtures. For instance, if we wanted to flag our entire test fixture as long-running (without having to mark each and every test method), we could do so.

```
Line 1   using NUnit.Framework;
    -    using NUnit.Core;
    -
    -    [TestFixture, Category("Long")]
    5    public class TestShortestPath2 {
    -
    -      [Test]
    -      public void Use50Cities() {
    -        TSP tsp = new TSP(); // Load with default cities
   10        Assert.AreEqual(2300, tsp.ShortestPath(50));
    -      }
    -
    -      [Test]
    -      public void Use100Cities() {
   15        TSP tsp = new TSP(); // Load with default cities
    -        Assert.AreEqual(4675, tsp.ShortestPath(100));
    -      }
    -
    -      [Test]
   20      public void Use150Cities() {
    -        TSP tsp = new TSP(); // Load with default cities
    -        Assert.AreEqual(5357, tsp.ShortestPath(150));
    -      }
    -
   25    }
```

TestShortestPath2.cs

Now you can quickly exclude the whole fixture using a category name.

Per-method Setup and Teardown

Each test should run independently of every other test; this allows you to run any individual test at any time, in any order.

To accomplish this feat, you may need to reset some parts of the testing environment in between tests, or clean up after a test has run. NUnit lets you specify two methods to set up and then tear down the test's environment using attributes:

```
[SetUp]
public void MySetup() {
  ...
}

[TearDown]
public void MyTeardown() {
  ...
}
```

In this example, the method `MySetup()` is called before each one of the `[Test]` methods is executed, and the method `MyTeardown()` is called after each test method is executed.

For example, suppose you needed some sort of database connection object for each test. Rather than including code in each test method that connects to and disconnects from the database, you could simply use setup and teardown methods.

```
[TestFixture]
public class TestDB {
  private Connection dbConn;

  [SetUp]
  public void MySetup() {
    dbConn = new Connection("oracle", 1521, user, pw);
    dbConn.Connect();
  }

  [TearDown]
  public void MyTeardown() {
    dbConn.Disconnect();
    dbConn = null;
  }

  [Test]
  public void TestAccountAccess() {
    // Uses dbConn
    ...
    ...
  }

  [Test]
  public void TestEmployeeAccess() {
    // Uses dbConn
    ...
    ...
  }
}
```

```
1. OneTimeSetup()
2.     MySetup()
3.         test method 1
4.     MyTeardown()
5.     MySetup()
6.         test method 2
7.     MyTeardown()
8. OneTimeTeardown()
```

Per-method setup runs before each test method, and teardown runs after each method.

One-time setup runs at start of all tests, and teardown runs at very end.

Figure 3.3: EXECUTION ORDER OF SETUP CODE

In this example, the method `MySetup()` will be called before `TestAccountAccess()`. After `TestAccountAccess()` has finished, `MyTearDown()` will be called. `MySetup()` will be called again, followed by `TestEmployeeAccess()` and then `MyTeardown()` again.

Per-class Setup and Teardown

Normally per-method setup is all you need, but in some circumstances you may need to set something up or clean up after the *entire* test class has run; for that, you need per-class setup and teardown (the difference between per-test and per-class execution order is shown in Figure 3.3 on this page). All you need to do is annotate your setup methods with the following attributes:

```
[TestFixtureSetUp]
public void OneTimeSetup() {
  . . .
}
[TestFixtureTearDown]
public void OneTimeTeardown() {
  . . .
}
```

Note that you can use both per-class and per-test methods in the same class.

3.5 NUnit Custom Asserts

The standard asserts that NUnit provides are usually sufficient for most testing. However, you may run into a situation where it would be handy to have your own, customized asserts. Perhaps you've got a special data type, or a common sequence of actions that is done in multiple tests.

The worst thing you can do is slavishly copy the same sequence of test code over and over again.

"Copy and paste" of common code in the tests can be a fatal disease. Instead, tests should be written to the same high standards as regular code, which means honoring good coding practices such as the DRY principle,[1] decoupling, orthogonality, and so on. Factor out common bits of test harness into real methods, and use those methods in your test cases.

Don't be afraid to write your own assertion-style methods. For instance, suppose you are testing a financial application and virtually all of the tests use a data type called Money.

```
using System;
using NUnit.Framework;
public class MoneyAssert {
  /**
   * Assert that the amount of money is an even
   * number of dollars (no cents)
   */
  public static void AssertNoCents(Money amount,
                                   String message) {
    Assert.AreEqual(
        amount.AsDecimal(),
        Decimal.Truncate(amount.AsDecimal()),
        message);
  }
  /**
   * Assert that the amount of money is an even
   * number of dollars (no cents)
   */
  public static void AssertNoCents(Money amount) {
    AssertNoCents(amount, "");
  }
}
```

MoneyAssert.cs

---

[1]DRY stands for "Don't Repeat Yourself." It's a fundamental technique that demands that every piece of knowledge in a system must have a single, unambiguous, and authoritative representation [HT00].

Note that we provide both forms of assert: one that takes a `string` and one that does not. Note also that we didn't copy any code in doing so; we merely forward the call on.

Now any other test classes in the project that need to test Money can use our own custom assertion method.

```
using NUnit.Framework;
[TestFixture]
public class TestSomething {
  [Test]
  public void CountDeMonet() {
    Money m = new Money(42.00);
    m.Add(2);
    MoneyAssert.AssertNoCents(m);
  }
}
```

TestSomething.cs

3.6 NUnit and Exceptions

We might be interested in two different kinds of exceptions:

1. Expected exceptions resulting from a test

2. Unexpected exceptions from something that's gone horribly wrong

Contrary to what you might think, exceptions are really good things—they tell us that something is wrong. Sometimes in a test, we *want* the method under test to throw an exception. Consider a method named `ImportList()`. It's supposed to throw an `ArgumentException` if passed a null list. We must test for that explicitly.

To test for expected exceptions, NUnit provides the [ExpectedException] attribute:

```
[TestFixture]
public class TestException {
  [Test, ExpectedException(typeof(ArgumentException))]
  public void TestForException() {
    WhitePages.ImportList(null);
    // Shouldn't get to here
  }
}
```

TestException.cs

This test method is now expected to throw an exception (from the call to `ImportList()`). If it doesn't, the test will fail. If the exception fires as expected, the test passes. Note that once the expected exception fires, any remaining code in the test method will be skipped.

In general, you should test a method for every expected exception, and make sure that the method throws it when it should. That covers us for expected exceptions, but what about unexpected exceptions?

NUnit will take care of those for you. For instance, suppose you are reading a file of test data. Rather than catching the possible I/O exceptions yourself, just let them propagate out to the test framework.

```
[Test]
public void TestData1() {
    StreamReader sr = new StreamReader( "data.txt");
    ...
}
```

The NUnit framework will catch any thrown exception and report it as an error, without any extra effort on your part. Even better, NUnit will report the *entire* stack trace right down to the bug itself, not just to some failed assert, which helps when trying to figure out why a test failed.

3.7 Temporarily Ignoring Tests

Normally, you want all tests to pass all of the time. But suppose you've thought up a bunch of tests first, written them, and are now working your way through implementing the code required to pass the tests. What about all those new tests that would fail now?

You can go ahead and write these tests, but you don't want the testing framework to run these tests just yet. NUnit provides the [Ignore] attribute:

```
[Test, Ignore("Not ready to test this yet")]
public void TestSomething() {
    ...
}
```

NUnit will report that this method was skipped (and show a yellow bar in the GUI version), so that you won't forget about it later.

In other testing frameworks and languages, you'd have to either name the method differently or comment it out. When using JUnit in Java, for instance, methods whose names start with "`test`" (as in `testSomething`) will be run as tests; you have to name the method something else until you're ready to tackle it. In any language, the code still has to compile cleanly; if it's not ready for that yet, then you should comment out the offending parts.

What you want to avoid at all costs is the habit of *ignoring* failing test results.

Now that you've got a good idea of *how* to write tests, it's time to take a closer look at figuring out *what* to test.

Chapter 4

What to Test: The Right-BICEP

It can be hard to look at a method or a class and try to come up with all the ways it might fail; to anticipate all the bugs that might be lurking in there. With enough experience, you start to get a feel for those things that are "likely to break," and can effectively concentrate on testing in those areas first. But without a lot of experience, it can be hard and frustrating trying to discover possible failure modes. End-users are quite adept at finding our bugs, but that's both embarrassing and damaging to our careers! What we need are some guidelines, some reminders of areas that might be important to test.

Let's take a look at six specific areas to test that will strengthen your testing skills, using your RIGHT-BICEP:

- **Right** — Are the results **right**?

- **B** — Are all the **boundary** conditions CORRECT?

- **I** — Can you check **inverse** relationships?

- **C** — Can you **cross-check** results using other means?

- **E** — Can you force **error conditions** to happen?

- **P** — Are **performance** characteristics within bounds?

4.1 Are the Results Right?

Right BICEP
The first and most obvious area to test is simply to see if the expected results are right—to validate the results.

We've seen simple data validation already: the tests in Chapter 2 that verify that a method returns the largest number from a list.

These are usually the "easy" tests, and many of these sorts of validations may even be specified in the requirements. If they aren't, you'll probably need to ask someone. You need to be able to answer the key question:

If the code ran correctly, how would I know?

If you cannot answer this question satisfactorily, then writing the code—or the test—may be a complete waste of time. "But wait," you may say, "that doesn't sound very agile! What if the requirements are vague or incomplete? Does that mean we can't write code until all the requirements are firm?"

No, not at all. If the requirements are truly not yet known, or complete, you can always invent some as a stake in the ground. They may not be correct from the user's point of view, but you now know what *you* think the code should do, and so you can answer the question.

Of course, you must then arrange for feedback with users to fine-tune your assumptions. The definition of "correct" may change over the lifetime of the code in question, but at any point, you should be able to prove that it's doing what you think it ought.

Using Data Files

For sets of tests with large amounts of test data, you might want to consider putting the test values and/or results in a separate data file that the unit test reads in. This doesn't need to be a very complicated exercise—and you don't even need to use XML.[1] Figure 4.1 on the next page is a version of `TestLargest` that reads in all of the tests from a data file.

---

[1] This is clearly a joke. XML is mandatory on all projects today, isn't it?

```csharp
using System;
using System.IO;
using System.Collections;
using NUnit.Framework;

[TestFixture]
public class TestLargestDataFile {

  /* Run all the tests in testdata.txt (does not test
   * exception case). We'll get an error if any of the
   * file I/O goes wrong.
   */

  [Test]
  public void TestFromFile() {
    String line;
    StreamReader rdr =
      new StreamReader("../../testdata.txt");

    while ((line = rdr.ReadLine()) != null) {
      if (line.StartsWith("#")) { // Ignore comments
        continue;
      }

      String[] tokens = line.Split(null);

      // Get the expected value
      String val = tokens[0];
      int expected = Int32.Parse(val);

      // And the arguments to Largest
      ArrayList argument_list = new ArrayList();

      for (int i=1; i < tokens.Length; i++) {
        argument_list.Add(Int32.Parse(tokens[i]));
      }

      // Convert to native array
      int[] args = (int[])argument_list.ToArray(
                                typeof(int));

      // And run the assert
      Assert.AreEqual(expected,
        Cmp.Largest(args));
    }
  }
}
```

Figure 4.1: TESTLARGESTDATAFILE: READING TEST SPECIFI-
CATIONS FROM A FILE.

The data file has a very simple format; each line contains a set of numbers. The first number is the expected answer, the numbers on the rest of the line are the arguments with which to test. We'll allow a pound-sign (#) for comments, so that you can put meaningful descriptions and notes in the test file.

The test file can then be as simple as:

```
#
# Simple tests:
#
9 7 8 9
9 9 8 7
9 9 8 9
#
# Negative number tests:
#
-7 -7 -8 -9
-7 -8 -7 -8
-7 -9 -7 -8
#
# Mixture:
#
7 -9 -7 -8 7 6 4
9 -1 0 9 -7 4
#
# Boundary conditions:
#
1 1
0 0
2147483647 2147483647
-2147483648 -2147483648
```

For just a handful of tests, as in this example, it's probably not worth the effort. But say this was a more advanced application, with tens or even hundreds of test cases in this form. Then the data file approach becomes a very compelling choice.

Be aware that test data, whether it's in a file or in the test code itself, might well be incorrect. In fact, experience suggests that test data is *more likely* to be incorrect than the code you're testing, especially if the data was hand-calculated or obtained from a system we're replacing (where new features may deliberately cause new results). When test data says you're wrong, double- and triple-check that the test data is right before attacking the code.

Something else to think about: the code as presented does not test any exception cases. How might you implement that?

Do whatever makes it easiest for you to prove that the method is right.

4.2 Boundary Conditions

In the previous "largest number" example, we discovered several boundary conditions: when the largest value was at the
end of the array, when the array contained a negative number,
an empty array, and so on.

Right **B** *ICEP*

Identifying boundary conditions is one of the most valuable
parts of unit testing, because this is where most bugs generally live—at the edges. Some conditions you might want to
think about:

- Totally bogus or inconsistent input values, such as a file
  name of `"!*W:X\&Gi/w~>g/h#WQ@"`.

- Badly formatted data, such as an e-mail address without
  a top-level domain (`"fred@foobar."`).

- Empty or missing values (such as 0, 0.0, `""`, or `null`).

- Values far in excess of reasonable expectations, such as
  a person's age of 10,000 years.

- Duplicates in lists that shouldn't have duplicates.

- Ordered lists that aren't, and vice-versa. Try handing a
  pre-sorted list to a sort algorithm, for instance—or even
  a reverse-sorted list.

- Things that arrive out of order, or happen out of expected
  order, such as trying to print a document before logging
  in, for instance.

An easy way to think of possible boundary conditions is to
remember the acronym CORRECT. For each of these items,
consider whether or not similar conditions may exist in your
method that you want to test, and what might happen if these
conditions were violated:

- **C**onformance — Does the value conform to an expected
  format?

- **O**rdering — Is the set of values ordered or unordered as
  appropriate?

- **R**ange — Is the value within reasonable minimum and
  maximum values?

- **R**eference — Does the code reference anything external that isn't under direct control of the code itself?

- **E**xistence — Does the value exist (e.g., is non-null, non-zero, present in a set, etc.)?

- **C**ardinality — Are there exactly enough values?

- **T**ime (absolute and relative) — Is everything happening in order? At the right time? In time?

We'll examine all of these boundary conditions in the next chapter.

4.3   Check Inverse Relationships

Right B $\boxed{I}$ *CEP*

Some methods can be checked by applying their logical inverse. For instance you might check a method that calculates a square root by squaring the result, and testing that it is tolerably close to the original number:

```
[Test]
public void SquareRootUsingInverse() {
  double x = MyMath.SquareRoot(4.0);
  Assert.AreEqual(4.0, x*x, 0.0001);
}
```

You might check that some data was successfully inserted into a database by then searching for it, and so on.

Be cautious when you've written both the original routine and it's inverse, as some bugs might be masked by a common error in both routines. Where possible, use a different source for the inverse test. In the square root example, we're just using regular multiplication to test our method. For the database search, we'll probably use a vendor-provided search routine to test our insertion.

4.4   Cross-check Using Other Means

Right BI $\boxed{C}$ *EP*

You might also be able to cross-check results of your method using different means.

Usually there is more than one way to calculate some quantity; we might pick one algorithm over the others because it performs better, or has other desirable characteristics. That's the one we'll use in production, but we can use one of the other versions to cross-check our results in the test system. This technique is especially helpful when there's a proven, known way of accomplishing the task that happens to be too slow or too inflexible to use in production code.

We can use that somewhat lesser version to our advantage to check that our new super-spiffy version is producing the same results:[2]

```
[Test]
public void SquareRootUsingStd() {
  double number = 3880900.0;
  double root1 = MyMath.SquareRoot(number);
  double root2 = Math.Sqrt(number);
  Assert.AreEqual(root2, root1, 0.0001);
}
```

TestRoots.cs

Another way of looking at this is to use different pieces of data from the class itself to make sure they all "add up." For instance, suppose you were working on a library's database system (that is, a brick-and-mortar library that lends out real books). In this system, the number of copies of a particular book should always balance. That is, the number of copies that are checked out plus the number of copies sitting on the shelves should always equal the total number of copies in the collection. These are separate pieces of data, and may even be reported by objects of different classes, but they still have to agree, and so can be used to cross-check one another.

4.5   Force Error Conditions

In the real world, errors happen. Disks fill up, network lines   *Right BIC* **E** *P*
drop, e-mail goes into a black hole, and programs crash. You should be able to test that your code handles all of these real-world problems by forcing errors to occur.

That's easy enough to do with invalid parameters and the like, but to simulate specific network errors—without unplugging

---

[2]Some spreadsheet engines (as found in Microsoft Excel™, etc.) employ similar techniques to check that the models and methods chosen to solve a particular problem are appropriate, and that the answers from different applicable methods agree with each other.

any cables—takes some special techniques. We'll discuss one way to do this using Mock Objects in Chapter 6 on page 73.

But before we get there, consider what kinds of errors or other environmental constraints you might introduce to test your method? Make a short list before reading further.

Think about this for a moment before reading on...

Here are a few environmental things we've thought of.

- Running out of memory
- Running out of disk space
- Issues with wall-clock time
- Network availability and errors
- System load
- Limited color palette
- Very high or very low video resolution

4.6 Performance Characteristics

Right BICE $\boxed{P}$

One area that might prove beneficial to examine is performance characteristics—not performance itself, but trends as input sizes grow, as problems become more complex, and so on.

What we'd like to achieve is a quick regression test of performance characteristics. All too often, we might release one version of the system that works okay, but somehow by the next release it has become dead-dog slow. We don't know why, or what change was made, or when, or who did it, or anything. And the end users are screaming bloody murder.

To avoid that awkward scenario, you might consider some rough tests just to make sure that the performance curve remains stable. For instance, suppose we've written a filter that identifies web sites that we wish to block (using our new product to view naughty pictures might get us in all sorts of legal trouble, after all.)

The code works fine with a few dozen sample sites, but will it work as well with 10,000? 100,000? Let's write a unit test to find out.

```
[Test]
public void FilterRanges() {
   Timer timer = new Timer();
   String naughty_url = "http://www.xxx.xxx.com";
   // First, check a bad URL against a small list
   URLFilter filter = new URLFilter(small_list);
   timer.Start();
   filter.Check(naughty_url);
   timer.End();
   Assert.IsTrue(timer.ElapsedTime < 1.0);
   // Next, check a bad URL against a big list
   filter = new URLFilter(big_list);
   timer.Start();
   filter.Check(naughty_url);
   timer.End();
   Assert.IsTrue(timer.ElapsedTime < 2.0);
   // Finally, check a bad URL against a huge list
   filter = new URLFilter(huge_list);
   timer.Start();
   filter.Check(naughty_url);
   timer.End();
   Assert.IsTrue(timer.ElapsedTime < 3.0);
}
```

TestFilter.cs

This gives us some assurance that we're still meeting performance targets. But because this one test takes 6–7 seconds to run, we may not want to run it every time. As long as we run it nightly or every couple of days, we'll quickly be alerted to any problems we may introduce, while there is still time to fix them.

Chapter 5

CORRECT
Boundary Conditions

Many bugs in code occur around "boundary conditions," that is, under conditions where the code's behavior may be different from the normal, day-to-day routine.

For instance, suppose you have a function that takes two integers:

```
public int Calculate(int a, int b) {
  return a / (a+b);
}
```

TestRoots.cs

Most of the time, this code will return a number just as you expect. But if the sum of a and b happens to equal zero, you will get a `DivideByZeroException` instead of a return value. That is a boundary condition—a place where things might suddenly go wrong, or at least behave differently from your expectations.

To help you think of tests for boundary conditions, we'll use the acronym CORRECT:

- **C**onformance — Does the value conform to an expected format?

- **O**rdering — Is the set of values ordered or unordered as appropriate?

- **R**ange — Is the value within reasonable minimum and maximum values?

- **R**eference — Does the code reference anything external that isn't under direct control of the code itself?

- **E**xistence — Does the value exist (e.g., is non-null, non-zero, present in a set, etc.)?

- **C**ardinality — Are there exactly enough values?

- **T**ime (absolute and relative) — Is everything happening in order? At the right time? In time?

Let's look at each one of these in turn. Remember that for each of these areas, you want to consider data that is passed in as arguments to your method as well as internal data that you maintain inside your method and class.

The underlying question that you want to answer fully is:

What else *can go wrong*?

Once you think of something that could go wrong, write a test for it. Once that test passes, again ask yourself, "what else can go wrong?" and write another test, and so on.

5.1 Conformance

C|ORRECT

Many times you expect or produce data that must conform to some specific format. An e-mail address, for instance, isn't just a simple string. You expect that it must be of the form:

```
name@somewhere.com
```

With the possibility of extra dotted parts:

```
firstname.lastname@subdomain.somewhere.com
```

And even oddballs like this one:

```
firstname.lastname%somewhere@subdomain.somewhere.com
```

Suppose you are writing a method that will extract the user's name from their e-mail address. You'll expect that the user's name is the portion before the "@" sign. What will your code do if there *is* no "@" sign? Will it work? Throw an exception? Is this a boundary condition you need to consider?[1]

Validating formatted string data such as e-mail addresses, phone numbers, account numbers, or file names is usually straightforward. But what about more complex structured data? Suppose you are reading some sort of report data that contains a header record linked to some number of data records, and finally to a trailer record. How many conditions might we have to test?

- What if there's no header, just data and a trailer?

- What if there's no data, just a header and trailer?

- What if there's no trailer, just a header and data?

- What if there's just a trailer?

- What if there's just a header?

- What if there's just data?

Just as with the simpler e-mail address example, you have to consider what will happen if the data does not conform to the structure you think it should.

And of course, if you are creating something like an e-mail address (possibly building it up from different sources) or the structured data above, you want to test your result to make sure it conforms.

5.2 Ordering

Another area to consider is the order of data, or the position of one piece of data within a larger collection. For instance, in the Largest() example in the previous chapter, one bug manifested itself depending on whether the largest number you were searching for was at the beginning or end of the list. C o RRECT

That's one aspect of ordering. Any kind of search routine should be tested for conditions where the search target is first or last, as many common bugs can be found that way.

---

[1]E-mail addresses are actually very complicated. A close reading of RFC822 may surprise you.

For another aspect of ordering, suppose you are writing a method that is passed a collection containing a restaurant order. You would probably expect that the appetizers will appear first in the order, followed by the salad (and that all-important dressing choice), then the entree and finally a decadent dessert involving lots of chocolate.

What happens to your code if the dessert is first, and the entree is last?

If there's a chance that sort of thing can happen, **and** if it's the responsibility of your method to deal with it if it does, then you need to test for this condition and address the problem. Now, it may be that this is not something your method needs to worry about. Perhaps this needs to be addressed at the user input level (see "Testing Invalid Parameters" later on).

If you're writing a sort routine, what might happen if the set of data is already ordered? Or worse yet, sorted in precisely reverse order? Ask yourself if that could cause trouble—if these are conditions that might be worth testing, too.

If you are supposed to maintain something in order, check that it is. For example, if your method is part of the GUI that is sending the dinner order back to the kitchen, you should have a test that verifies that the items are in the correct serving order:

```
[Test]
public void KitchenOrder() {
  Order order = new Order();
  FoodItem dessert = new Dessert("Chocolate Decadence");
  FoodItem entree = new Entree("Beef Oscar");
  FoodItem salad  = new Salad("Parmesan Peppercorn");

  // Add out of order
  order.AddFoodItem(dessert);
  order.AddFoodItem(entree);
  order.AddFoodItem(salad);

  // But should come out in serving order
  IEnumerator itr = order.GetEnumerator();

  Assert.AreEqual(salad, itr.Current);
  itr.MoveNext();
  Assert.AreEqual(entree, itr.Current);
  itr.MoveNext();
  Assert.AreEqual(dessert, itr.Current);
  itr.MoveNext();

  // No more left
  Assert.IsFalse(itr.MoveNext());
}
```

Of course, from a human factors standpoint, you'd need to modify the code so that it's flexible enough to allow people to eat their ice cream first, if so desired. In which case, you'd need to add a test to prove that your four-year old nephew's ice cream comes with everyone else's salads, but Grandma's ice cream comes at the end with your cappuccino.

5.3 Range

Range is a convenient catch-all word for the situation where a variable's type allows it to take on a wider range of values than you need—or want. For instance, a person's age is typically represented as an integer, but no one has ever lived to be 200,000 years old, even though that's a perfectly valid integer value. Similarly, there are only 360 degrees in a circle, even though degrees are commonly stored in an integer.

CO **R** RECT

In good object oriented design, you do not use a raw native type (e.g., an int or Int32) to store a bounded-integer value such as an age, or a compass heading.

```csharp
using System;
//
// Compass bearing
//
public class Bearing {
  protected int bearing; // 0..359
  //
  // Initialize a bearing to a value from 0..359
  //
  public Bearing(int num_degrees) {
    if (num_degrees < 0 || num_degrees > 359) {
      throw new ArgumentException("Bad bearing");
    }
    bearing = num_degrees;
  }
  //
  // Return the angle between our bearing and another.
  // May be negative.
  //
  public int AngleBetween(Bearing anOther) {
    return bearing - anOther.bearing;
  }
}
```

Bearing.cs

Notice that the angle returned is just an int, as we are not placing any range restrictions on the result (it may be negative, etc.)

By encapsulating the concept of a bearing within a class, you've now got one place in the system that can filter out bad data. You cannot create a `Bearing` object with out of range values. Thus, the rest of the system can use `Bearing` objects and be assured that they contain only reasonable values.

Other ranges may not be as straightforward. For instance, suppose you have a class that maintains two sets of *x, y* coordinates. These are just integers, with arbitrary values, but the constraint on the range is such that the two points must describe a rectangle with no side greater than 100 units. That is, the allowed range of values for both *x, y* pairs is interdependent. You'll want a range test for any method that can affect a coordinate to ensure that the resulting range of the *x, y* pairs remains legitimate. For more information on this topic, see "invariants" in the Design Issues chapter on page 117.

Since you will likely call this from a number of different tests, it probably makes sense to make a new assert method:

```
public const int MAX_DIST = 100;
static public void AssertPairInRange(Point one,
                                     Point two,
                                     String message) {
  Assert.IsTrue(Math.Abs(one.X - two.X) <= MAX_DIST,
                message);
  Assert.IsTrue(Math.Abs(one.Y - two.Y) <= MAX_DIST,
                message);
}
```

But the most common ranges you'll want to test probably depend on physical data structure issues, not application domain constraints. Take a simple example like a stack class that implements a stack of `Strings` using an array:

```
public class MyStack {
  public MyStack() {
    stack = new String[100];
    nextIndex = 0;
  }
  public String Pop() {
    return stack[--nextIndex];
  }
  // Delete n items from the stack en-masse
  public void Delete(int n) {
    nextIndex -= n;
  }
  public void Push(String aString) {
    stack[nextIndex++] = aString;
  }
}
```

TestPair.cs

```
   public String Top() {
     return stack[nextIndex-1];
   }
   private int nextIndex;
   private String[] stack;
}
```

MyStack.cs

There are some potential bugs lurking here, as there are no checks at all for either an empty stack or a stack overflow. However we manipulate the index variable nextIndex, one thing is supposed to be always true: (next_index >= 0 && next_index < stack.Length). We'd like to check to make sure this expression is true.

Now both nextIndex and stack are private variables; you don't want to have to expose those just for the sake of testing. There are several ways around this problem; for now we'll just make a special method in Stack named CheckInvariant():

```
   public void CheckInvariant() {
     if (!(nextIndex >= 0 &&
           nextIndex < stack.Length)) {

       throw new InvariantException(
               "nextIndex out of range: " + nextIndex +
               " for stack length " + stack.Length);

     }
   }
```

MyStack.cs

Now a test method can call CheckInvariant() to ensure that nothing has gone awry inside the guts of the stack class, without having direct access to those same guts.

```
   using NUnit.Framework;

   [TestFixture]
   public class TestMyStack {

     [Test]
     public void Empty() {
       MyStack stack = new MyStack();
       stack.CheckInvariant();
       stack.Push("sample");
       stack.CheckInvariant();
       // Popping last element ok
       Assert.AreEqual("sample", stack.Pop());
       stack.CheckInvariant();
       // Delete from empty stack
       stack.Delete(1);
       stack.CheckInvariant();
     }
   }
```

TestMyStack.cs

When you run this test, you'll quickly see that we need to add some range checking!

```
TestCase 'TestMyStack.Empty' failed: InvariantException
nextIndex out of range: -1 for stack length 100
        mystack.cs(34,0): at MyStack.CheckInvariant()
        testmystack.cs(20,0): at TestMyStack.Empty()
```

It's much easier to find and fix this sort of error here in a simple testing environment instead of buried in a real application.

Almost any indexing concept (whether it's a genuine integer index or not) should be extensively tested. Here are a few ideas to get you started:

- Start and End index have the same value

- First is greater than Last

- Index is negative

- Index is greater than allowed

- Count doesn't match actual number of items

- ...

5.4 Reference

COR **R** ECT

What things does your method reference that are outside the scope of the method itself? Any external dependencies? What state does the class have to have? What other conditions must exist in order for the method to work?

For example, a method in a web application to display a customer's account history might require that the customer is first logged on. The method Pop() for a stack requires a non-empty stack. Shifting the transmission in your car to Park from Drive requires that the car is stopped.

If you have to make assumptions about the state of the class and the state of other objects or the global application, then you need to test your code to make sure that it is well-behaved if those conditions are not met. For example, the code for the microprocessor-controlled transmission might have unit tests that check for that particular condition: the state of the transmission (whether it can shift into Park or not) depends on the state of the car (is it in motion or stopped).

```
[Test]
public void JamItIntoPark() {
  transmission.Shift(DRIVE);
  car.AccelerateTo(35);
  Assert.AreEqual(DRIVE, transmission.CurrentGear);

  // should silently ignore
  transmission.Shift(PARK);
  Assert.AreEqual(DRIVE, transmission.CurrentGear);

  car.AccelerateTo(0); // i.e., stop
  car.BrakeToStop();

  // should work now
  transmission.Shift(PARK);
  Assert.AreEqual(PARK, transmission.CurrentGear);
}
```

The *preconditions* for a given method specify what state the world must be in for this method to run. In this case, the precondition for putting the transmission in park is that the car's engine (a separate component elsewhere in the application's world) must be at a stop. That's a documented requirement for the method, so we want to make sure that the method will behave gracefully (in this particular case, just ignore the request silently) in case the precondition is not met.

At the end of the method, *postconditions* are those things that you guarantee your method will make happen. Direct results returned by the method are one obvious thing to check, but if the method has any side-effects then you need to check those as well. In this case, applying the brakes has the side effect of stopping the car.

Some languages even have built-in support for preconditions and postconditions; interested readers might want to read about Eiffel in *Object-Oriented Software Construction* [Mey97].

5.5 Existence

A large number of potential bugs can be discovered by asking the key question "does some given thing exist?". *CORR* **E** *CT*

For any value you are passed in or maintain, ask yourself what would happen to the method if the value didn't exist—if it were null, or blank, or zero.

Many C# library methods will throw an exception of some sort when faced with non-existent data. The problem is that it's hard to debug a generic runtime exception buried deep in some library. But an exception that reports "Age isn't set" makes tracking down the problem much easier.

Most methods will blow up if expected data is not available, and that's probably **not** what you want them to do. So you test for the condition—see what happens if you get a `null` instead of a `CustomerRecord` because some search failed. See what happens if the file doesn't exist, or if the network is unavailable.

Ah, yes: things in the environment can wink out of existence as well—networks, files' URLs, license keys, users, printers— you name it. All of these things may not exist when you expect them to, so be sure to test with plenty of nulls, zeros, empty strings and other nihilist trappings.

Make sure your method can stand up to nothing.

5.6 Cardinality

CORREcT

Cardinality has nothing to do with either highly-placed religious figures or small red birds, but instead with counting.

Computer programmers (your humble authors included) are really bad at counting, especially past 10 when the fingers can no longer assist us. For instance, answer the following question quickly, off the top of your head, without benefit of fingers, paper, or UML:

> If you've got 12 feet of lawn that you want to fence, and each section of fencing is 3 feet wide, how many fence posts do you need?

If you're like most of us, you probably answered "4" without thinking too hard about it. Pity is, that's wrong—you need five fence posts as shown in Figure 5.1 on page 66. This model, and the subsequent common errors, come up so often that they are graced with the name "fence post errors."

It's one of many ways you can end up being "off by one;" an occasionally fatal condition that afflicts all programmers from time to time. So you need to think about ways to test how well your method counts, and check to see just how many of a thing you may have.

It's a related problem to Existence, but now you want to make sure you have exactly as many as you need, or that you've made exactly as many as needed. In most cases, the count of some set of values is only interesting in these three cases:

1. Zero
2. One
3. More than one

It's called the "0–1–n Rule," and it's based on the premise that if you can handle more than one of something, you can probably handle 10, 20, or 1,000 just as easily. Most of the time that's true, so many of our tests for cardinality are concerned with whether we have 2 or more of something. Of course there are situations where an exact count makes a difference—10 might be important to you, or 250.

Suppose you are maintaining a list of the Top-Ten food items ordered in a pancake house. Every time an order is taken, you have to adjust the top-ten list. You also provide the current top-ten list as a real-time data feed to the pancake boss's PDA. What sort of things might you want to test for?

- Can you produce a report when there aren't yet ten items in the list?

- Can you produce a report when there are no items on the list?

- Can you produce a report when there is only one item on the list?

- Can you add an item when there aren't yet ten items in the list?

- Can you add an item when there are no items on the list?

- Can you add an item when there is only one item on the list?

- What if there aren't ten items on the menu?

- What if there are no items on the menu?

Having gone through all that, the boss now changes his mind and wants a top-twenty list instead. What do you have to change?

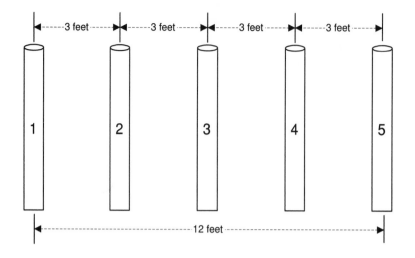

Figure 5.1: A SET OF FENCE POSTS

The correct answer is "one line," something like the following:

```
public MaxEntries {
   get { return 20; }
}
```

Now, when the boss gets overwhelmed and pleads with you to change this to be a top-five report (his PDA is pretty small, after all), you can go back and change this one number. The test should automatically follow suit, because it uses the same property.

So in the end, the tests concentrate on boundary conditions of 0, 1, and n, where n can—and will—change as the business demands.

5.7 Time

CORREC T

The last boundary condition in the CORRECT acronym is Time. There are several aspects to time you need to keep in mind:

- Relative time (ordering in time)
- Absolute time (elapsed and wall clock)
- Concurrency issues

Some interfaces are inherently stateful; you expect that Lo-gin() will be called before Logout(), that PrepareState-ment() is called before ExecuteStatement(), Connect() before Read() which is before Close(), and so on.

What happens if those methods are called out of order? Maybe you should try calling methods out of the expected order. Try skipping the first, last and middle of a sequence. Just as order of data may have mattered to you in the earlier examples (as we described in "Ordering" on page 57), now it's the order of the calling sequence of methods.

Relative time might also include issues of timeouts in the code: how long your method is willing to wait for some ephemeral resource to become available. As we'll discuss shortly, you'll want to exercise possible error conditions in your code, including things such as timeouts. Maybe you've got conditions that aren't guarded by timeouts—can you think of a situation where the code might get "stuck" waiting forever for something that might not happen?

This leads us to issues of elapsed time. What if something you are waiting for takes "too much" time? What if your method takes too much time to return to the caller?

Then there's the actual wall clock time to consider. Most of the time, this makes no difference whatsoever to code. But every now and then, time of day will matter, perhaps in subtle ways. Here's a quick question, true or false: every day of the year is 24 hours long?

The answer is *"it depends."* In UTC (Universal Coordinated Time, the modern version of Greenwich Mean Time, or GMT), the answer is YES. In areas of the world that do not observe Daylight Savings Time (DST), the answer is YES. In most of the U.S. (which does observe DST), the answer is NO. In April, you'll have a day with 23 hours (spring forward) and in October you'll have a day with 25 (fall back). This means that arithmetic won't always work as you expect; 1:45AM plus 30 minutes might equal 1:15, for instance.

But you've tested any time-sensitive code on those boundary days, right? For locations that honor DST and for those that do not?

Oh, and don't assume that any underlying library handles these issues correctly on your behalf. Unfortunately, when it comes to time, there's a lot of broken code out there.

Finally, one of the most insidious problems brought about by time occurs in the context of concurrency and synchronized access issues. It would take an entire book to cover designing, implementing, and debugging multi-threaded, concurrent programs, so we won't take the time now to go into details, except to point out that most code you write in most languages today **will** be run in a multi-threaded environment.

So ask yourself, what will happen if multiple threads use this same object at the same time? Are there global or instance-level data or methods that need to be synchronized? How about external access to files or hardware? Be sure to add the `lock` keyword to any data element or method that needs it, and try firing off multiple threads as part of your test.

5.8 Try It Yourself

Now that we've covered the Right-BICEP and CORRECT way to come up with tests, it's your turn to try.

For each of the following examples and scenarios, write down as many possible unit tests as you can think of.

Exercises

Answer on 148

1. **A simple stack class.** Push `String` objects onto the stack, and `Pop` them off according to normal stack semantics. This class provides the following methods:

```
using System;
public interface StackExercise {
    /// <summary>
    /// Return and remove the most recent item from
    /// the top of the  stack.
    /// </summary>
    /// <exception cref="StackEmptyException">
    /// Throws exception if the stack is empty.
    /// </exception>
    String Pop();

    /// <summary>
    /// Add an item to the top of the stack.
    /// </summary>
```

```
/// <param name="item">A String to push
/// on the stack</param>
void Push(String item);

/// <summary>
/// Return but do not remove the most recent
/// item from the top of the stack.
/// </summary>
/// <exception cref="StackEmptyException">
/// Throws exception if the stack is empty.
/// </exception>
String Top();

/// <summary>
/// Returns true if the stack is empty.
/// </summary>
bool IsEmpty();
}
```

StackExercise.cs

Here are some hints to get you started: what is likely to break? How should the stack behave when it is first initialized? After it's been used for a while? Does it really do what it claims to do?

2. **A shopping cart.** This class lets you add, delete, and count the items in a shopping cart.

Answer on 149

What sort of boundary conditions might come up? Are there any implicit restrictions on what you can delete? Are there any interesting issues if the cart is empty?

```
public interface ShoppingCart {
    /// <summary>
    /// Add this many of this item to the
    /// shopping cart.
    /// </summary>
    /// <exception cref="NegativeCountException">
    /// </exception>
    void AddItems(Item anItem, int quantity);

    /// <summary>
    /// Delete this many of this item from the
    /// shopping cart
    /// </summary>
    /// <exception cref="NegativeCountException">
    /// </exception>
    /// <exception cref="NoSuchItemException">
    /// </exception>
    void DeleteItems(Item anItem, int quantity);

    /// <summary>
    /// Count of all items in the cart
    /// (that is, all items x qty each)
    /// </summary>
    int ItemCount { get; }

    /// Return iterator of all items
    IEnumerable GetEnumerator();
}
```

ShoppingCart.cs

Answer
on 150

3. **A fax scheduler.** This code will send faxes from a specified file name to a U.S. phone number. There is a validation requirement; a U.S. phone number with area code must be of the form *xnn-nnn-nnnn*, where *x* must be a digit in the range [2..9] and *n* can be [0..9]. The following blocks are reserved and are not currently valid area codes: *x*11, *x*9*n*, 37*n*, 96*n*.

The method's signature is:

```
///
/// Send the named file as a fax to the
/// given phone number.
/// <exception cref="MissingOrBadFileException">
/// </exception>
/// <exception cref="PhoneFormatException">
/// </exception>
/// <exception cref="PhoneAreaCodeException">
/// </exception>
public bool SendFax(String phone, String filename)
```

Given these requirements, what tests for boundary conditions can you think of?

Answer
on 151

4. **An automatic sewing machine that does embroidery.** The class that controls it takes a few basic commands. The co-ordinates (0,0) represent the lower-left corner of the machine. *x* and *y* increase as you move toward the upper-right corner, whose coordinates are x = TableSize.Width - 1 and y = TableSize.Height - 1.

Coordinates are specified in fractions of centimeters.

```
public void MoveTo(double x, double y);
public void SewTo(double x, double y);
public void SetWorkpieceSize(double width,
                            double height);
public Size WorkpieceSize { get; }
public Size TableSize { get; }
```

There are some real-world constraints that might be interesting: you can't sew thin air, of course, and you can't sew a workpiece bigger than the machine.

Given these requirements, what boundary conditions can you think of?

Answer
on 152

5. **Audio/Video Editing Transport.** A class that provides methods to control a VCR or tape deck. There's the notion of a "current position" that lies somewhere between the beginning of tape (BOT) and the end of tape (EOT).

You can ask for the current position and move from there to another given position. *Fast-forward* moves from current position toward EOT by some amount. *Rewind* moves from current position toward BOT by some amount.

When tapes are first loaded, they are positioned at BOT automatically.

```csharp
using System;

public interface AVTransport {
    /// Move the current position ahead by this many
    /// seconds. Fast-forwarding past end-of-tape
    /// leaves the position at end-of-tape
    void FastForward(double seconds);

    /// Move the current position backwards by this
    /// many seconds. Rewinding past zero leaves
    /// the position at zero
    void Rewind(double seconds);

    /// Return current time position in seconds
    double CurrentTimePosition();

    /// Mark the current time position with label
    void MarkTimePosition(String name);

    /// Change the current position to the one
    /// associated with the marked name
    void GotoMark(String name);
}
```

AVTransport.cs

6. **Audio/Video Editing Transport, Release 2.0.** As above, but now you can position in seconds, minutes, or frames (there are exactly 30 frames per second in this example), and you can move relative to the beginning or the end.

Answer on 153

Chapter 6

Using Mock Objects

The objective of unit testing is to exercise just one method at a time, but what happens when that method depends on other things—hard-to-control things such as the network, or a database, or even the latest Microsoft stock price?

What if your code depends on other parts of the system—maybe even *many* other parts of the system? If you're not careful, you might find yourself writing tests that end up initializing nearly every system component just to give the tests enough context in which to run. Not only is this time consuming, it also introduces a ridiculous amount of coupling into the testing process: someone goes and changes an interface or a database table, and suddenly the setup code for your poor little unit test dies mysteriously. Even the best-intentioned developers will become discouraged after this happens a few times, and eventually may abandon all testing. But there are techniques we can use to help.

In movie and television production, crews will often use *stand-ins* or *doubles* for the real actors. In particular, while the crews are setting up the lights and camera angles, they'll use *lighting doubles*: inexpensive, unimportant people who are about the same height and complexion as the expensive, important actors lounging safely in their luxurious trailers.

The crew then tests their setup with the lighting doubles, measuring the distance from the camera to the stand-in's nose, adjusting the lighting until there are no unwanted shadows, and so on, while the obedient stand-in just stands there and doesn't whine or complain about "lacking motivation" for their character in this scene.

So what we're going to do in unit testing is similar to the use of lighting doubles in the movies: we'll use a cheap stand-in that is kind of close to the real thing, at least superficially, but that will be easier to work with for our purposes.

6.1 Simple Stubs

What we need to do is to stub out all those uncooperative parts of the rest of the real world and replace each of them with a more complicit ally—our own version of a "lighting double." For instance, perhaps we don't want to test against the real database, or with the real, current, wall-clock time. Let's look at a simple example.

Suppose throughout your code you call your own Now property to return the current date and time. It might be defined to look something like this:

```
public DateTime Now {
  get {
    return DateTime.Now;
  }
}
```

(In general, we usually suggest wrapping calls to facilities outside the scope of the application to better encapsulate them—and this is a good example.) Since the concept of current time is wrapped in code of your own writing, you can easily change it to make debugging a little easier:

```
public DateTime Now {
  get {
    if (DEBUG)
      return currentTime;
    else
      return DateTime.Now;
  }
}
```

You might then have other debug routines to manipulate the system's idea of "current time" to cause events to happen that you'd have to wait around for otherwise.

SystemEnvironment.cs

Examples.cs

This is one way of stubbing out the real functionality, but it's messy. First of all, it only works if the code consistently calls your own Now and does not call DateTime.Now directly. What we need is a slightly cleaner—and more object-oriented—way to accomplish the same thing.

6.2 Mock Objects

Fortunately, there's a testing pattern that can help: *mock objects*. A mock object is simply a debug replacement for a real-world object. There are a number of situations that come up where mock objects can help us. Tim Mackinnon [MFC01] offers the following list:

- The real object has nondeterministic behavior (it produces unpredictable results, like a stock-market quote feed.)

- The real object is difficult to set up.

- The real object has behavior that is hard to trigger (for example, a network error).

- The real object is slow.

- The real object has (or is) a user interface.

- The test needs to ask the real object about how it was used (for example, a test might need to confirm that a callback function was actually called).

- The real object does not yet exist (a common problem when interfacing with other teams or new hardware systems).

Using mock objects, we can get around all of these problems. The three key steps to using mock objects for testing are:

1. Use an interface to describe the object

2. Implement the interface for production code

3. Implement the interface in a mock object for testing

The code under test only ever refers to the object by its interface, so it can remain blissfully ignorant as to whether it is using the real object or the mock. Let's take another look at our time example. We'll start by creating an interface for a number of real-world environmental things, one of which is the current time:

```
public interface Environmental {
  DateTime Now {
    get;
  }
  // Other methods omitted...
}
```

Next, we create the real implementation:

```
public class SystemEnvironment : Environmental {
  public DateTime Now {
    get {
      return DateTime.Now;
    }
  }
}
```

And finally, the mock implementation:

```
using System;
public class MockSystemEnvironment : Environmental {
  private DateTime currentTime;
  public MockSystemEnvironment(DateTime when) {
    currentTime = when;
  }
  public DateTime Now {
    get {
      return currentTime;
    }
  }
  public void IncrementMinutes(int minutes) {
    currentTime = currentTime.AddMinutes(minutes);
  }
}
```

Note that in the mock implementation, we pass the `DateTime` to be used as the initial current value to the constructor, and the constructor tucks this away in an instance variable. This is the value we'll return when we're asked for the current time. We also provide a method `IncrementMinutes` which adds the given number of minutes to this time. This allows you to control date and time returned by the mock object.

Now suppose we've written an application with a new method, `Reminder()`, which plays the "go home" whistle if called after 5pm. (Fans of the Flintstones will remember that this was

Fred's cue to jump from the cab and surf down the back of his dinosaur). Among other things, this method depends on the Now property. Some details are omitted, but the part we're interested in looks like this:

```
using System;

public class Checker {
   Environmental env;

   public Checker(Environmental env) {
      this.env = env;
   }

   public void Reminder() {
      DateTime now = env.Now;

      if (now.Hour >= 17) {
         env.PlayWavFile( "quit_whistle.wav");
      }
   }
}
```

Line numbers: Line 1, 5, 10, 15

Checker.cs

In the production environment—the real world code that gets shipped to customers—an object of this class would be initialized by passing in a real SystemEnvironment. The test code, on the other hand, uses a MockSystemEnvironment.

The code under test that uses env.Now doesn't know the difference between a test environment and the real environment, as they both implement the same interface. You can now write tests that exploit the mock object by setting the time to known values and checking for the expected behavior.

In addition to the Now property that we've shown, the Environmental interface also supports a PlayWavFile() method call (used on line 14 in Checker.cs above). With a bit of extra support code in our mock object, we can also add tests to see if the PlayWavFile() method was called without having to listen to the computer's speaker.

```
private bool soundWasPlayed = false;
public void PlayWavFile(string fileName) {
   soundWasPlayed = true;
}
// For convenience, check the sound played
// flag and reset it in one method call
public bool CheckAndResetSound() {
   bool value = soundWasPlayed;
   soundWasPlayed = false;
   return value;
}
```

MockSystemEnvironment.cs

Putting all of this together, a test using this setup would go something like this:

```
using System;
using NUnit.Framework;

[TestFixture]
public class TestChecker {

  [Test]
  public void QuittingTime() {

    DateTime when = new DateTime(2004,10,1,16,55,0);
    MockSystemEnvironment env;
    env = new MockSystemEnvironment(when);
    Checker checker = new Checker(env);

    // No alarm sounds at 16:55
    checker.Reminder();
    Assert.IsFalse(env.CheckAndResetSound(), "16:55");

    // Now try 17:00
    env.IncrementMinutes(5);
    checker.Reminder();
    Assert.IsTrue(env.CheckAndResetSound(), "17:00");

    // And finally 19:00
    env.IncrementMinutes(120);
    checker.Reminder();
    Assert.IsTrue(env.CheckAndResetSound(), "19:00");
  }
}
```

Line numbers: Line 1, 5, 10, 15, 20, 25

TestChecker.cs

The code creates a `DateTime` object containing the time to be used for our first test, and passes that object to a new mock system environment that we'll use to run the tests.

On line 16 we can run the `Reminder()` call, which will (unwittingly) use the mock environment. The `Assert.IsFalse()` call on the next line checks that the .wav file has *not* been played yet, as it is not yet quitting time in the mock object environment. But we'll fix that in short order; line 20 puts the mock time exactly equal to quitting time (a good boundary condition, by the way). We then call the `Reminder()` method again, This time, the sound should have been played, so we call `Assert.IsTrue` on line 22 to make sure that the .wav file did play this time around.

Finally, we'll test the `Reminder()` method one more time, setting the mock clock forward by two hours. Notice how easy it is to alter and check conditions in the mock environment—you don't have to bend over and listen to the PC's speaker, or reset the clock, or pull wires, or anything like that.

Because we've got an established interface to all system functions, people will (hopefully) be more likely to use it instead of calling things such as `DateTime.Now()` directly, and we now have control over the behavior behind that interface.

And that's all there is to mock objects: fake out parts of the real world so you can concentrate on testing your own code.

6.3 Formalizing Mock Objects

In the old days, just having the ability to call subroutines was a great advance. Then libraries of code became popular—everything had to be library. Nowadays, libraries aren't good enough. You've got to have a *framework* to be taken seriously.

In the case of .NET, there are several alternative mock object frameworks to choose from (a good list can be found at `http://www.mockobjects.org`). In this section we'll look at one of these, DotNetMock.[1]

The DotNetMock framework is actually three things in one:

1. It's a framework (not surprisingly), allowing you to create mock objects in a structured way.

2. It contains a (small) set of predefined mock objects that you can use out of the box to test your application.

3. Finally, it comes with a technology, dynamic mocks, that let's you construct mock objects without all that messy coding.

Let's look at each of these in turn. But before we do, it's worth noting that because we're in .NET's CLR environment, this same framework can be used to mock objects for any .NET language.

DotNetMock Framework

When you think about it, there's really not too much to a mock object: it's simply some object that implements a particular interface, returns values you want it to return, and which

---

[1]`http://sourceforge.net/projects/dotnetmock`

allows you to check that it was used in a certain way. As a result, the basic frameworks for creating mock objects are also correspondingly simple.

To illustrate this, let's look at using the DotNetMock framework to help us test an access control library. We'll start with a pretty trivial class, `AccessController`. Each `AccessController` object is responsible to controlling access to a particular resource—we give the name of the resource to the constructor. To determine if a particular user can use the resource, we call the object's `CanAccess()` method, passing in the user's name and password. The code for this class might look something like this:

```
using System;
public class AccessController {
  private ILogger logger;
  private String  resource;
  public AccessController(String resource,
                          ILogger logger) {
    this.logger = logger;
    this.resource = resource;
    logger.SetName("AccessControl");
  }

  public bool CanAccess(String user, String password) {
    logger.Log("Checking access for " + user +
               " to " + resource);

    if (password == null || password.Length == 0) {
      logger.Log("Missing password. Access denied");
      return false;
    }
    // more checks...
    logger.Log("Access granted");
    return true;
  }
}
```

AccessController.cs

We'd like to test this access control code, but notice that it's calling some external logger object. This isn't a major problem: the logger is called via an interface.

```
using System;
public interface ILogger {
  void SetName(String name);
  void Log(String msg);
}
```

ILogger.cs

We can mock up that interface pretty easily: we just need to implement two methods, one used to set the name of the thing doing the logging, and the other to log the actual messages.

```
using System;
public class MockLogger1 : ILogger {
  public void SetName(String name) {
  }
  public void Log(String msg) {
  }
}
```

Given this, we can now write a basic unit test. For our first test, we'll check that the access controller correctly denies access if we don't pass in a password.

```
using System;
using NUnit.Framework;
[TestFixture]
public class TestAccessController {

  [Test]
  public void MissingPassword1() {
    MockLogger1 logger = new MockLogger1();
    AccessController access =
      new AccessController("secrets", logger);
    Assert.IsFalse(access.CanAccess("dave", null));
    Assert.IsFalse(access.CanAccess("dave", ""));
  }
}
```

However, this test does not verify that our access controller is logging the correct messages. This is where the mock objects framework might help—one of its main features is that it makes it easy to manage *expectations*:[2] the framework makes it easy to record things that we expect to happen, and then to verify that they actually *did* happen.

To start with, let's extend our mock object to verify that the access controller is correctly setting its name into the logger. We do this by adding expectations to our MockLogger class.

```
using System;
using DotNetMock;
public class MockLogger2 : MockObject, ILogger {
  private ExpectationValue _name =
    new ExpectationValue("name");
  // Mock control interface
  public String ExpectedName {
    set { _name.Expected = value; }
  }
```

---

[2]We clearly need more frameworks like this to help us deal with some of our more demanding end users.

```
        // Implement ILogger interface
        public void SetName(String name) {
            _name.Actual = name;
        }
        public void Log(String msg) {
        }
    }
```

A couple of things have changed. First, we now use the Dot-NetMock namespace, and have our MockLogger extend the MockObject class. To get this to compile, we've also added a reference to DotNetMock.dll to our project. This DLL is available in the DotNetMock package at the SourceForge URL given previously.

Next, we've added an ExpectationValue instance variable to our class. An expectation is basically a variable that holds two values: its expected value and its actual, current value. At the end of running a test, we can call a Verify method, and the mock objects framework checks that the expected and actual values in all the expectation objects match. If they do, our code must have worked as expected. If not, Verify raises an assertion error, and the unit test fails.

Third, we need to provide a way of setting the expected and actual values. The actual value is set via the standard ILog-ger SetName() method: when a caller invokes SetName(), we need to change the value associated with the name.

To set the expected value, though, we need a new method—one that's not part of the ILogger interface. We provide an accessor called ExpectedName to allow us to set this.

With this all in place, we can now test that the access controller is correctly setting its name into the logger object.

```
[Test]
public void MissingPassword2() {
    MockLogger2 logger = new MockLogger2();
    logger.ExpectedName = "AccessControl";
    AccessController access =
        new AccessController("secrets", logger);
    Assert.IsFalse(access.CanAccess("dave", null));
    logger.Verify();
}
```

Note how this test sets the expected value of the logger's name into the mock logger object before creating the access controller. After the test runs, it then calls the mock object's `Verify()` method to confirm that the actual value agrees with this expectation. Running the test, we get our green line: all is well.

However, we're still not testing that the access controller is writing the correct messages to the logger: we're hoping that it will say "Checking access for dave to secrets," followed by "Missing password. Access denied." Here we have an expectation that has two values. Fortunately, the framework gives us expectation collection classes to deal with this. We'll update our mock logger to use them.

```
Line 1   using System;
     -   using DotNetMock;

     -   public class MockLogger3 : MockObject, ILogger {

     5
     -     private ExpectationValue _name =
     -         new ExpectationValue("name");

     -     private ExpectationArrayList _msgs =
    10         new ExpectationArrayList("msgs");

     -     // Mock control interface

     -     public String ExpectedName {
    15       set { _name.Expected = value; }
     -     }

     -     public void AddExpectedMsg(String msg) {
     -       _msgs.AddExpected(msg);
    20     }

     -     // Implement ILogger interface
     -     public void SetName(String name) {
     -       _name.Actual = name;
    25     }

     -     public void Log(String msg) {
     -       _msgs.AddActual(msg);
     -     }
    30   }
```

MockLogger3.cs

At line 9 we've created a new expectation collection called _msgs. As with an `ExpectationValue`, this holds both actual and expected values; it just allows us to hold a number of both. The method `AddExpectedMsg` at line 18 lets us add to the list of expected values, and we change the actual `Log` call to add to the list of actual values.

Now we can change the test to verify that the correct log messages are generated.

TestAccessController.cs

```
[Test]
public void MissingPassword3() {
  MockLogger3 logger = new MockLogger3();
  logger.ExpectedName = "AccessControl";
  logger.AddExpectedMsg(
    "Checking access for dave to secrets");
  logger.AddExpectedMsg(
    "Missing password. Access denied");
  AccessController access =
    new AccessController("secrets", logger);
  Assert.IsFalse(access.CanAccess("dave", null));
  logger.Verify();
}
```

Note that we've added two calls to AddExpectedMsg(). When Verify() is called at the end of the test, the mock logger will check that the access controller actually logged exactly these messages.

Sometimes a mock object has to be able to handle a larger number of calls. For example, you might want to verify that a sales reporting method iterates over all 50 states in the United States without actually having to add each state by name to an ExpectationArrayList. Fortunately, the framework implements an ExpectationCounter class. You can set an expected count value, and then invoke its Inc() method to increment the actual counter.

Supplied Mock Objects

One of the nice things about using a standardized framework for testing is that you can start to build a library of standard mock objects and reuse these across projects. In fact, in the open source world, you might even find that other folks have mocked up the interfaces that you need and made them freely available. The DotNetMock package actually comes with a (small) number of these off-the-shelf mock object packages, available in DotNetMock.Framework. Here we'll look at one of these, Data, which implements many of the interfaces in .NET's System.Data.

Let's start by implementing more of our access controller. After verifying that a password has been supplied, we'll now go to a database table and verify that a row exists giving this user, identified with the given password, access to our resource.

NUnit's Built-in Mocks

NUnit 2.2 includes a built-in, lightweight, dynamic mock object facility. See the documentation that comes with NUnit for full details, but the built-in system has the following features:

- Dynamically create a default mock implementation of any interface or `MarshalByReference` class

- Allow arbitrary calls, or reject any method calls that weren't explicitly expected

- Expect that methods will be called in the given order

- Expect that a method will *not* be called

- Specify the return value for a method called with a particular set of arguments, or for any arbitrary arguments

- Specify an exception to be thrown for a method called with a particular set of arguments, or for any arbitrary arguments

- Override `DynamicMock` in order to provide a custom implementation for any method

If you'd like to experiment with mock objects without having to download and learn a larger, more fully-featured product, then this might be the perfect place to start.

```csharp
using System;
using System.Data;
using System.Data.SqlClient;
public class AccessController1 {
  private ILogger        logger;
  private String         resource;
  private IDbConnection conn;

  public static readonly String CHECK_SQL =
    "select count(*) from access where " +
    "user=@user and password=@password " +
    "and resource=@resource";

  public AccessController1(String resource,
                           ILogger logger,
                           IDbConnection conn) {
    this.logger   = logger;
    this.resource = resource;
    this.conn     = conn;
    logger.SetName("AccessControl");
  }

  public bool CanAccess(String user, String password) {
    logger.Log("Checking access for " + user +
      " to " + resource);

    if (password == null || password.Length == 0) {
      logger.Log("Missing password. Access denied");
      return false;
    }

    IDbCommand cmd = conn.CreateCommand();
    cmd.CommandText = CHECK_SQL;
    cmd.Parameters.Add(
      new SqlParameter("@user",     user));
    cmd.Parameters.Add(
      new SqlParameter("@password", password));
    cmd.Parameters.Add(
      new SqlParameter("@resource", resource));
    IDataReader rdr = cmd.ExecuteReader();

    int rows = 0;

    if (rdr.Read())
      rows = rdr.GetInt32(0);

    cmd.Dispose();

    if (rows == 1) {
      logger.Log("Access granted");
      return true;
    }
    else {
      logger.Log("Access denied");
      return false;
    }
  }
}
```

AccessController1.cs

The test code for this is somewhat more complicated than the previous cases, mostly because we want to knit together all the various objects used to access the database (the connection, the command, various parameters, and the reader that returns the result). We also want to set up a reasonable set of expectations to ensure that the underlying code is calling the database layer correctly.

```
Line 1    using System;
    -     using NUnit.Framework;
    -     using DotNetMock.Framework.Data;

    5     [TestFixture]
    -     public class TestAccessController1 {
    -       [Test]
    -       public void TestValidUser() {
    -         MockLogger3 logger = new MockLogger3();
    10         logger.ExpectedName = "AccessControl";
    -         logger.AddExpectedMsg(
    -           "Checking access for dave to secrets");
    -         logger.AddExpectedMsg("Access granted");

    15         // set up the mock database
    -         MockDbConnection conn = new MockDbConnection();
    -         MockCommand cmd = new MockCommand();
    -         MockDataReader rdr = new MockDataReader();

    20         conn.SetExpectedCommand(cmd);
    -         cmd.SetExpectedCommandText(
    -           AccessController1.CHECK_SQL);
    -         cmd.SetExpectedExecuteCalls(1);
    -         cmd.SetExpectedParameter(
    25           new MockDataParameter("@user",     "dave"));
    -         cmd.SetExpectedParameter(
    -           new MockDataParameter("@password", "shhh"));
    -         cmd.SetExpectedParameter(
    -           new MockDataParameter("@resource", "secrets"));
    30
    -         cmd.SetExpectedReader(rdr);
    -         object [,] rows = new object[1,1];
    -         rows[0, 0] = 1;
    -         rdr.SetRows(rows);
    35
    -         AccessController1 access =
    -           new AccessController1("secrets", logger, conn);
    -         Assert.IsTrue(access.CanAccess("dave", "shhh"));
    -         logger.Verify();
    40         conn.Verify();
    -         cmd.Verify();
    -       }
    -     }
```

TestAccessController1.cs

On line 3 we bring in the DotNetMock framework's `Data` components. In the body of the test method, we start by creating and setting up a mock logger as before. At line 16 we create three mock database objects: the connection, a command (used to issue SQL queries into the database), and a reader (used to return the results of a query).

We now need to associate these three objects together. Line 20 tells the connection object that when it is asked to generate a

> ### It isn't all perfect
>
> Observant readers may be wondering why our new AccessController class went to the trouble of using a `Reader` object to get the count back from executing the query. Why didn't we just use the `ExecuteScalar` method of the command object to return the count directly?
>
> Unfortunately, the mock object implementation of `IDbCommand` isn't quite complete (at least at the time of writing). Although `ExecuteScalar` is implemented, it always returns a `null` value. This means that we couldn't use it in our tests.

command object it should return our mock command object, cmd. We then set up that command object's expectations: the SQL it should receive, the number of times it will be executed, and the parameters it should expect to receive.

Line 31 starts the stanza that sets up the reader object. It is first associated with the command (so that when the mock command is executed it will return this reader object). We then set up its result set, a two dimensional array of objects, containing the rows returned by the query and the columns in each row. In our case, the result set contains just a single row containing a single column, the count, but we still need to wrap it in the two-dimensional array.

Finally, on line 36, we create our access controller and check to see if "dave" can access the resource "secrets" by using the password "shhh." Because these values correspond to the values we set up for the query, the access controller will be able to use our mock database objects, which will return a count of "1" and the access will be accepted. At the end of the test, we then verify that the logger, connection, and command mock objects were used correctly by our method under test.

Dynamic Mock Objects

There'll be times when you need to test something that uses an existing interface and there are no pre-written mock objects lying around. Often, you can just jump right on in and create a new mock object. But what if the interface that you're mocking is enormous, with dozens of methods and accessors? That could mean a lot of work producing a mock object that implements the interface. This is particularly galling if you only need one or two methods from the interface to run your tests.

This is where dynamic mock objects come in. They let you create an object that responds as if it implemented a full interface, but in reality it is totally generic. You only need to tell this object how to respond to the method calls that your code uses. This can represent a considerable saving in time. It'll also give you less code to maintain in the future.

To make this more concrete, let's imagine we have an application that has something to do with customers. At some point, a developer created a monstrous ICustomer interface which defines a whole bunch of accessors to get to information about a customer. It looks something like this.

```
using System;
public interface ICustomer {
    String  Title          { get; }
    String  FirstName      { get; }
    String  MiddleInitial  { get; }
    String  LastName       { get; }
    String  NameSuffix     { get; }
    String  SSN            { get; }
    Address HomeAddress    { get; }
    Address WorkAddress    { get; }
    Date    FirstContacted { get; }
    Date    LastContacted  { get; }
    int     ContactCount   { get; }
    // and so on, and so on, for 30 more accessors
}
```
ICustomer.cs

Our current job is to implement a class that can generate mail to these customers. As part of that task, we need to be able to generate both long and short forms of the greeting (so our mail could say "Mr Joe Smith, III" on the envelope and "Dear Mr Smith" on the letter). Our code looks something like this.

```csharp
using System;
using System.Text;
public class Mailer {
  private ICustomer customer;
  public Mailer(ICustomer customer) {
    this.customer = customer;
  }
  public String ShortGreeting() {
    return customer.Title + " " + customer.LastName;
  }
  public String FullGreeting() {
    StringBuilder result = new StringBuilder();
    Append(result, customer.Title);
    Append(result, customer.FirstName);
    Append(result, customer.MiddleInitial);
    Append(result, customer.LastName);
    if (customer.NameSuffix.Length > 0)
      result.Append(", " + customer.NameSuffix);
    return result.ToString();
  }
  private void Append(StringBuilder result,
                      String field) {
    if (field != null && field.Length > 0)
      if (result.Length > 0)
        result.Append(" ");
    result.Append(field);
  }
}
```

Mailer.cs

To test this code, we'd need to create some kind of customer object and pass it to our routine. This could be a lot of work, because the interface is fairly large. This is where dynamic mock objects can help.

The dynamic mock packages[3] operate by creating *proxy objects*. These are objects that are designed to stand in for their real-world counterparts. In the dynamic mock object context, this means that we can use a proxy in place of a real object in our tests. However, we still need to be able to control this generated proxy object—we need to be able to tell it how to respond. This is where the controller comes in.

The controller is in charge of a dynamic mock object. You use the controller to create an instance of the mock, and to tell the

---

[3]There are two that we've come across at the time of writing. One, which we'll show here, comes with the DotNetMock framework. The other is NMock (http://nmock.truemesh.com/). The two share much underlying code, although the NMock API differs slightly from the DotNetMock one.

mock what do do. In the code that follows, the controller is the object of type `IMock`, created on line 13. On the next line, we tell the controller to create the actual mock object—the object that implements the `ICustomer` interface.

```
Line 1    using System;
    -     using DotNetMock.Dynamic;
    -     using NUnit.Framework;

    5
    -     [TestFixture]
    -     public class TestCalculator {

    -       [Test]
   10       public void AgeCalculation() {
    -         IMock mock =
    -           new DynamicMock(typeof(ICustomer));
    -         ICustomer customer = (ICustomer)mock.Object;
   15         mock.SetValue( "Title",         "Mr. ");
    -         mock.SetValue( "FirstName",     "Fred");
    -         mock.SetValue( "MiddleInitial", "E");
    -         mock.SetValue( "LastName",      "Bloggs");
    -         mock.SetValue( "NameSuffix",    "III");
   20
    -         Mailer mailer = new Mailer(customer);
    -         Assert.AreEqual( "Mr.  Bloggs",
    -                           mailer.ShortGreeting());
    -         Assert.AreEqual( "Mr.  Fred E Bloggs, III",
   25                           mailer.FullGreeting());
    -       }
    -     }
```

TestMailer.cs

Once we have the controller, we can also program up the way we want the mock object to behave. For the purposes of our test, that's pretty simple: we simply want it to return given values for the various components of the customer's name. The controller's `SetValue` calls starting on line 15 set that up. We then pass this mock-customer into the calculator and test some age calculations.

One of the key things to notice is that we didn't have to implement all the various methods in the `ICustomer` interface. Instead, we just set up the ones that we knew we were going to be using. This makes life a lot simpler, and is one of the key advantages of the dynamic mock style of testing.

You can do more with dynamic mock objects than merely set the return value of a method call. The various `Expect...` calls can be used to program a sequence of actions and responses into a mock object. The code that follows is somewhat artificial, but it illustrates some of the uses of `Expect`.

```
Line 1   using System;
    -    using NUnit.Framework;
    -    using DotNetMock.Dynamic;

    5    interface ITaxCalculator {
    -      decimal CalculateTax(decimal amount, String state);
    -    }

    -    public class ExpectExamples {
    10
    -      public ExpectExamples() {

    -        IMock mock = new DynamicMock(typeof(ITaxCalculator));

    15         mock.ExpectAndReturn("CalculateTax",7.25,100,"TX");
    -          mock.ExpectAndReturn("CalculateTax",7.00,100,"NC");
    -          mock.ExpectAndThrow("CalculateTax",
    -            new ArgumentOutOfRangeException(), 100, "XX");

    20         ITaxCalculator calc = (ITaxCalculator)mock.Object;

    -          // The following asserts simply illustrate
    -          // how the mock object would be used.
    -          // This is not a typical test.
    25         Assert.AreEqual(7.25,
    -                            calc.CalculateTax(100, "TX"));
    -          Assert.AreEqual(7.0,
    -                            calc.CalculateTax(100, "NC"));

    30         try {
    -            calc.CalculateTax(100, "XX");
    -            Assert.Fail("Should have thrown an exception");
    -          }
    -          catch (ArgumentOutOfRangeException) { ; }
    35
    -          mock.Verify();
    -      }
    -    }
```

The code creates a mock object for a (silly) sales tax calculator on line 13. The three lines starting on line 15 then program this mock object to expect three calls to the method `Calcu-lateTax()`. On the first call, the method should expect to be passed the parameters 100 and "TX", and should return the value 7.25. On the next call, it should return 7.0 after being passed 100 and "NC". On the last call, it should instead throw an `ArgumentOutOfRangeException`, because it will be passed an invalid state abbreviation ("XX").

Normally we'd then pass this mock object into some other object under test. However, to keep this example short, here we're just running some assertions against it directly. As we use the object, it verifies that the `CalculateTax()` method is indeed called three times, and that the expected parameters are passed in each time. It also causes the mock object to return the desired values (or throw the required exception) on each call.

6.4 When Not To Mock

Mock objects are an appealing technology, but because they involve writing code, they represent a definite cost to your project. Whenever you find yourself thinking that you want to write a mock object to help with testing, stop and consider alternatives for a couple of seconds. In particular, ask yourself the simple question: "do I need to write a mock object at all?" Sometimes you can eliminate the need for a mock object through some simple refactoring.

As a (somewhat contrived) example, let's imagine that we're writing code that downloads files to a handheld device over a relatively slow wire. Because of some hardware restrictions, after we've sent a block of data, we have to wait a while before trying to talk with the device again. The length of time we have to wait depends on the amount of data sent—the hardware guys gave us a table of values to use.

We might start off by writing a routine that waits a length of time dependent on the size of data sent:

```
public void WaitForData(int dataSize) {
  int timeToWait;
  if (dataSize < 100)
    timeToWait = 50;
  else if (dataSize < 250)
    timeToWait = 100;
  else if (dataSize < 600)
    timeToWait = 150;
  else
    timeToWait = 200;
  Thread.Sleep(timeToWait);
}
```

Example.cs

Now we want to test this method, but there's a problem. The only way to see if it works is to check to see if it sleeps for the right amount of time for various values of the `dataSize` parameters. That's not an easy test to write: we'd have to build in a *fudge factor*, because the time we measure for the wait won't be exact. We might even have to set up some kind of watchdog thread to ensure that the sleep doesn't go on too long. There's also the elapsed time to consider: if running our tests causes `Thread.Sleep` to be called multiple times, our unit tests will take longer to complete—we won't be popular.

After reading this chapter, your first though might be to solve these problems using a mock object. If we replace `Thread` with some kind of mock object, we can verify that its `Sleep()` method was called with the expected values. Class `Thread` is not an interface, and even if it were, it has a boatload of properties and members.

This is the time to reflect: could we redesign our code slightly to make it easier to test? Of course we can!

```
public int HowLongToWait(int dataSize) {
  int timeToWait;
  if (dataSize < 100)
    timeToWait = 50;
  else if (dataSize < 250)
    timeToWait = 100;
  else if (dataSize < 600)
    timeToWait = 150;
  else
    timeToWait = 200;
  return timeToWait;
}
public void WaitForData(int dataSize) {
  Thread.Sleep(HowLongToWait(dataSize));
}
```

Example.cs

In this code we've split the waiting into two methods. One calculates the number of milliseconds to wait based on the data's size, and the other calls it to get the parameter to pass the `Thread.Sleep()`. If we assume that the framework `Sleep()` method works, then there's probably no need to test this second method: we can eyeball it and see it does what it says it should. That leaves us with the simple task of testing the method that calculates the time to wait.

```
[Test]
void WaitTimes() {
  Waiter w = new Waiter();
  Assert.AreEqual(50,  w.HowLongToWait(0));
  Assert.AreEqual(50,  w.HowLongToWait(99));
  Assert.AreEqual(100, w.HowLongToWait(100));
  Assert.AreEqual(100, w.HowLongToWait(249));
  Assert.AreEqual(150, w.HowLongToWait(250));
  Assert.AreEqual(150, w.HowLongToWait(599));
  Assert.AreEqual(200, w.HowLongToWait(600));
}
```

Example.cs

A simple refactoring has led us to a better design, and eliminated a whole lot of pain associated with coding up the tests.

Chapter 7

Properties of
Good Tests

Unit tests are very powerful magic, and if used badly can cause an enormous amount of damage to a project by wasting your time. If unit tests aren't written and implemented properly, you can easily waste so much time maintaining and debugging the tests themselves that the production code—and the whole project—suffers.

We can't let that happen; remember, the whole reason you're doing unit testing in the first place is to make your life easier! Fortunately, there are only a few simple guidelines that you need to follow to keep trouble from brewing on your project.

Good tests have the following properties, which makes them A-TRIP:

- **A**utomatic

- **T**horough

- **R**epeatable

- **I**ndependent

- **P**rofessional

Let's look at what each of these words means to us.

7.1 Automatic

-TRIP

Unit tests need to be run automatically. We mean "automatically" in at least two ways: invoking the tests and checking the results.

It must be really easy for you to invoke one or more unit tests, as you will be doing it all day long, day in and day out. So it really can't be any more complicated than pressing one button in the IDE or typing in one command at the prompt in order to run the tests you want. Some IDEs can even be set up to run the unit tests continually in the background.

It's important to maintain this environment: don't introduce a test that breaks the automatic model by requiring manual steps. Whatever the test requires (database, network connections, etc.), make these an automatic part of the test itself. Mock objects, as described in Chapter 6, can help insulate you from changes in the real environment.

But you're not the only one running tests. Somewhere a machine should be running all of the unit tests for all checked-in code continuously. This automatic, unattended check acts as a "back stop"; a safety mechanism to ensure that whatever is checked in hasn't broken any tests, anywhere. In an ideal world, this wouldn't be necessary as you could count on every individual developer to run all the necessary tests themselves.

But this isn't an ideal world. Maybe an individual didn't run some necessary test in a remote corner of the project. Perhaps they have some code on their own machine that makes it all work—but they haven't checked that code in, so even though the tests work on their own machine, those same tests fail everywhere else.

You may want to investigate systems such as Cruise Control[1] and other open source products that manage continuous building and testing.

Finally, by "automatic" we mean that the test must determine for itself whether it passed or failed. Having a person (you or some other hapless victim) read through the test output and

---

[1]http://ccnet.thoughtworks.com

determine whether the code is working or not is a recipe for project failure. It's an important feature of consistent regression to have the tests check for themselves. We humans aren't very good at those repetitive tasks, and besides we've got more important things to do—remember the project?

This idea of having the tests run by themselves and check themselves is critical, because it means that you don't have to *think* about it—it just happens as part of the project. Testing can then fulfill its role as a major component of our project's safety net. (Version control and automation are the other two major components of the "safety net.") Tests are there to catch you when you fall, but they're not in your way. You'll need all of your concentration as you cross today's high-wire.

7.2 Thorough

Good unit tests are thorough; they test everything that's likely   A-[*T*]*RIP*
to break. But just how thorough? At one extreme, you can aim to test every line of code, every possible branch the code might take, every exception it throws, and so on. At the other extreme, you test just the most likely candidates—boundary conditions, missing and malformed data, and so on. It's a question of judgment, based on the needs of your project.

If you want to aim for more complete coverage, then you may want to invest in code coverage tools to help. (For instance "NCover," `http://workspaces.gotdotnet.com/ncover`).

These tools can help you determine how much of the code under test is actually being exercised.

It's important to realize that bugs are not evenly distributed throughout the source code. Instead, they tend to clump together in problematic areas (for an interesting story along these lines, see the sidebar on the following page).

This phenomenon leads to the well-known battle cry of "don't patch it, rewrite it." Often, it can be much cheaper and less painful to throw out a piece of code that has a clump of bugs and rewrite it from scratch. And of course, it's much safer to rewrite code from scratch now: you'll have a set of unit tests that can confirm the new code works as it should.

Reported Bugs vs. Unit Test Coverage

We had a client recently that didn't quite believe in the power of unit tests. A few members of the team were very good and disciplined at writing unit tests for their own modules, many were somewhat sporadic about it, and a few refused to be bothered with unit tests at all.

As part of the hourly build process, we whipped up a simple Ruby script that performed a quick-and-dirty analysis of test coverage: it tallied up the ratio of test code asserts to production code methods for each module. Well-tested methods may have 3, 4, or more asserts each; untested methods will have none at all. This analysis ran with every build and produced a bar-graph, ranking the most-tested modules at the top and the untested modules at the bottom.

After a few weeks of gathering figures, we showed the bargraph to the project manager, without initial explanation. He was very surprised to see all of the "problem modules" lumped together at the bottom—he thought we had somehow produced this graph based on bug reports from QA and customer support. Indeed, the modules at the top of the graph (well tested) were nearly unknown to him; very few, if any, problems had ever been reported against them. But the clump of modules at the bottom (that had no unit tests) were *very* well known to him, the support managers, and the local drugstore which had resorted to stocking extra-large supplies of antacid.

The results were very nearly linear: the more unit-tested the code, the fewer problems.

7.3 Repeatable

Just as every test should be independent from every other   *A-T* **R** *IP*
test, they must be independent of the environment as well.
The goal remains that every test should be able to run over
and over again, in any order, *and produce the same results.*
This means that tests cannot rely on anything in the external
environment that isn't under your direct control.

Use mock objects as necessary to isolate the item under test
and keep it independent from the environment. If you are
forced to use some element from the real world (a database,
perhaps), make sure that you won't get interference from any
other developer. Each developer needs their own "sandbox"
to play in, whether that's their own database instance within
Oracle, or their own webserver on some non-standard port.

Without repeatability, you might be in for some surprises at
the worst possible moments. What's worse, these sort of surprises are usually bogus—it's not really a bug, it's just a problem with the test. You can't afford to waste time chasing down
phantom problems.

Each test should produce the same results every time. If it
doesn't, then that should tell you that there's a *real* bug in
the code.

7.4 Independent

Tests need to be kept neat and tidy, which means keeping   *A-TR* **I** *P*
them tightly focused, and independent from the environment
and each other (remember, other developers may be running
these same tests at the same time).

When writing tests, make sure that you are only testing one
thing at a time.

Now that doesn't mean that you use only one assert in a test,
but that one test method should concentrate on a single production method, or a small set of production methods that,
together, provide some feature.

Sometimes an entire test method might only test one small aspect of a complex production method—you may need multiple test methods to exercise the one production method fully.

Ideally, you'd like to be able to have a traceable correspondence between potential bugs and test code. In other words, when a test fails, it should be obvious where in the code the underlying bug exists.

Independent also means that no test relies on any other test; you should be able to run any individual test at any time, and in any order. You don't want to have to rely on any other test having run first.

We've shown mechanisms to help you do this: the per-test setup and teardown methods and the per-class setup and teardown methods. Use these methods to ensure that every test gets a fresh start—and doesn't impact any test that might run next.

Remember, you aren't guaranteed that NUnit tests will run in any particular order, and as you start combining tests and suites in ever-increasing numbers, you really can't afford to carry ordering dependencies along with you.

John Donne may have been right about people, but not about unit tests: every test *should be* an island.

7.5 Professional

A-TRI P

The code you write for a unit test is real; some may argue it's even more real than the code you ship to customers. This means that it must be written and maintained to the same professional standards as your production code. All the usual rules of good design—maintaining encapsulation, honoring the DRY principle, lowering coupling, etc.—must be followed in test code just as in production code.

It's easy to fall into the trap of writing very linear test code; that is, code that just plods along doing the same thing over and over again, using the same lines of code over and over again, with nary a function or object in sight. That's a bad thing. Test code must be written in the same manner as real code. That means you need to pull out common, repeated bits of code and put that functionality in a method instead, so it can be called from several different places.

You may find you accumulate several related test methods that should be encapsulated in a class. Don't fight it! Go ahead and create a new class, even if it's only ever used for testing. That's not only okay, it's encouraged: test code is real code. In some cases, you may even need to create a larger framework, or create a data-driven testing facility (remember the simple file reader for TestLargest on page 47?).

Don't waste time testing aspects that won't help you. Remember, you don't want to create tests just for the sake of creating tests. Test code must be thorough in that it must test everything interesting about a method that is likely to contain a bug. If it's not likely to contain a bug, don't bother testing it. That means that usually you shouldn't waste time testing things like simple property accessors:

```
public Money Balance {
  get { return balance; }
}
```

Frankly, there's just not much here to go wrong that the compiler can't catch. Testing methods such as these is just a waste of time. However, if the accessor is doing some work along the way, then suddenly it becomes interesting—and we will want to test it:

```
public Money Balance {
  get {
    return posted.GetBalance() -
        unposted.GetDebits() +
        unposted.GetCredits();
  }
}
```

That's probably worth testing.

Finally, expect that there will be at least as much test code written as there will be production code. Yup, you read that right. If you've got 20,000 lines of code in your product, then it would be reasonable to expect that there would be 20,000 lines or more of unit test code to exercise it. That's a lot of test code, which is partly why it needs to be kept neat and tidy, well designed and well-factored, just as professional as the production code.

7.6 Testing the Tests

There is one major conceptual weakness in our plans so far. Testing code to make sure it works is a great idea, but you have to write code to perform the tests. What happens when there are bugs in our test code? Does that mean you have to write test code to test the tests that test the code??? Where will it all end?

Fortunately, you don't need to go to that extreme. There are two things you can do to help ensure that the test code is correct:

- Improve tests when fixing bugs
- Prove tests by introducing bugs

How to Fix a Bug

The steps you take when fixing a bug are very important to unit testing. Many times, an existing test will expose a bug in the code, and you can then simply fix the code and watch the vigilant test pass.

When a bug is found "in the wild" and reported back, that means there's a hole in the net—a missing test. This is your opportunity to close the hole, and make sure that this bug never escapes again. All it takes is four simple steps:

1. Identify the bug.

2. Write a test that fails, to prove the bug exists.

3. Fix the code such that the test now passes.

4. Verify that *all* tests still pass (i.e., you didn't break anything else as a result of the fix).

This simple mechanism of applying real-world feedback to help improve the tests is very effective. Over time, you can expect that your test coverage will steadily increase, and the number of bugs that escape into the wild from existing code will decrease.

Of course, as you write new code, you'll undoubtedly introduce new bugs, and new classes of bugs, that aren't being

```
[Test]
public void Add() {
  // Create a new account object
  Account acct = new Account();
  // Populate with our test person
  acct.SetPerson(TEST_PERSON_1);
  // Add it to the database
  DatabaseHandler.Add(acct);
  // Should find it
  Assert.IsTrue(DatabaseHandler.Search(TEST_PERSON_1));
}
```

Figure 7.1: TEST ADDING A PERSON TO A DATABASE

caught by the tests. But when fixing any bug, ask yourself the key question:

Could this same kind of problem happen any-where else?

Then it doesn't matter whether you're fixing a bug in an older feature or a new feature; either way, apply what you've just learned to the *whole* project. Encode your new-found knowledge in all the unit tests that are appropriate, and you've done more than just fix one bug. You've caught a whole class of bugs.

Spring the Trap

If you're not sure that a test is written correctly, the easiest thing to do is to "spring the trap": cause the production code to exhibit the very bug you're trying to detect, and verify that the test fails as expected.

For instance, suppose you've got a test method that adds a customer account to the database and then tries to find it, something like the code in Figure 7.1. Perhaps you're not certain that the "finding" part is really working or not—it might be reporting success even if the record wasn't added correctly.

So maybe you'll go into the Add() method for Database-Handler and short-circuit it: just return instead of actually adding the record to the database. Now you should see the assertion fail, because the record has not been added.

But wait, you may cry, what about a leftover record from a previous test run? Won't that be in the database? No, it won't, for several reasons:

- You may not really be testing against a live database. The code exercised by the above test case lies between the add method shown and the actual low-level database calls. Those database calls may well be handled by a mock object, whose data is not held persistently in between runs.

- Tests are independent. All tests can be run in any order, and do not depend on each other, so even if a real database is part of this test, the setup and tear-down must ensure that you get a "clean sandbox" to play in. The attempt above to spring the trap can help prove that this is true.

Now the Extreme Programming folks claim that their disciplined practice of test-first development avoids the problem of poor tests that don't fail when they should. In test-first development, you only ever write code to fix a failing test. As soon as the test passes, then you know that the code you just added fixed it. This puts you in the position where you always know with absolute certainty that the code you introduced fixes the failing test that caused you to write the code in the first place.

But there's many a slip 'twixt the cup and the lip, and while test-first development does improve the situation dramatically, there will still be opportunities to be mislead by coincidences. For those occasions, you can satisfy any lingering doubts by deliberately "springing the trap" to make sure that all is as you expect.

Finally, remember to write tests that are A-TRIP (Automatic, Thorough, Repeatable, Independent, Professional); keep adding to your unit tests as new bugs and types of bugs are discovered; and check to make sure your tests really do find the bugs they target.

Then sit back and watch problems on your project disappear like magic.

Chapter 8

Testing on a Project

Up to now we've talked about testing as an individual, solitary exercise. But of course, in the real world you'll likely have teammates to work with. You'll all be unit testing together, and that brings up a couple of issues.

8.1 Where to Put Test Code

On a small, one-person project, the location of test code and encapsulation of the production code may not be very important, but on larger projects it can become a critical issue. There are several different ways of structuring your production and test code that we'll look at here.

In general, you don't want to break any encapsulation for the sake of testing (or as Mom used to say, "don't expose your privates!"). Most of the time, you should be able to test a class by exercising its public methods. If there is significant functionality that is hidden behind private or protected access, that might be a warning sign that there's another class in there struggling to get out. When push comes to shove, however, it's probably better to break encapsulation with working, tested code than it is to have good encapsulation of untested, non-working code.

Same directory

Suppose you are writing a class named:

```
com.pragprog.wibble.Account
```

with a corresponding test in:

```
com.pragprog.wibble.TestAccount
```

The first and easiest method of structuring test code is to simply include it right in the same project and assembly alongside the production code.

This has the advantage that `TestAccount` can access `internal` and `protected internal` member variables and methods of `Account`. But the disadvantage is that the test code is lying around, cluttering up the production code directory. This may or may not be a problem depending on your method of creating a release to ship to customers.

Most of the time, it's enough of a problem that we prefer one of the other solutions. But for small projects, this might be sufficient.

Separate Assemblies

The next option is to create your tests in a separate assembly from the production code.

This has the advantage of keeping a clean separation between code that you ship and code for testing.

The disadvantage is that now the test code is in a different assembly; You won't be able to access internal or protected internal members unless your test code uses a subclass of the production code that exposes the necessary members. For instance, suppose the class you want to test looks like this:

```
namespace FacilitiesManagment {
  public class Pool {
    protected Date lastCleaned;
    public void xxxx xx {
      xxx xxx xxxx;
    }
    ...
  }
}
```

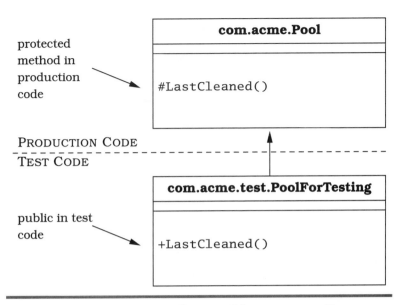

Figure 8.1: SUBCLASSES EXPOSE METHODS FOR TESTING

You need to get at that non-public bit of data that tells you when the pool was last cleaned for testing, but there's no accessor for it. (If there were, the pool association would probably sue us; they don't like to make that information public.) So you make a subclass that exposes it just for testing.

```
using FacilitiesManagment;
namespace FacilitiesManagmentTesting {
  public class PoolForTesting : Pool {
    public Date LastCleaned {
      get { return lastCleaned; }
    }
  }
}
```

You then use `PoolForTesting` in the test code instead of using `Pool` directly (see Figure 8.1). In fact, you could make this class private to the test code (to ensure that we don't get sued).

Whatever convention the team decides to adopt, make sure it does so consistently. You cannot have some of the tests in the system set up one way, and other tests elsewhere set up a different way. Pick a style that looks like it will work in your environment and stick with it for all of the system's unit tests.

8.2 Test Courtesy

The biggest difference between testing by yourself and testing with others lies in synchronizing working tests and code.

When working with other members of a team, you will be using some sort of version control system, such as Visual SourceSafe or CVS. (If you aren't familiar with version control, or would like some assistance in getting it set up and working correctly, please see [TH03].)

In a team environment (and even in a personal environment) you should make sure that when you check in code (or otherwise make it available to everyone) that it has complete unit tests, and that is passes all of them. In fact, every test in the whole system should continue to pass with your new code.

The rule is very simple: As soon as anyone else can access your code, all tests everywhere need to pass. Since you should normally work in fairly close synchronization with the rest of the team and the version control system, this boils down to **"all tests pass all the time."**

Many teams institute policies to help "remind" developers of the consequences of breaking the build, or breaking the tests. These policies might begin by listing potential infractions involving code that you have checked in (or otherwise made available to other developers):

- Incomplete code (e.g., checking in only one class file but forgetting to check in other files it may depend upon).

- Code that doesn't compile.

- Code that compiles, but breaks existing code such that existing code no longer compiles.

- Code without corresponding unit tests.

- Code with failing unit tests.

- Code that passes its own tests, but causes other tests elsewhere in the system to fail.

If found guilty of any of these heinous crimes, you may be sentenced to providing donuts for the entire team the next morning, or beer or soda, or frozen margaritas, or maybe you'll have to nursemaid the build machine, or some other token, menial task.

A little lighthearted law enforcement usually provides enough motivation against careless accidents. But what happens if you have to make an incompatible change to the code, or if you make a change that *does* cause other tests to fail elsewhere in the system?

The precise answer depends on the methodology and process you're using on the project, but somehow you need to coordinate your changes with the folks who are responsible for the other pieces of code—which may well be you! The idea is to make all of the necessary changes at once, so the rest of the team sees a coherent picture (that actually works) instead of a fragmented, non-functional "work in progress." (For more information on how to use version control to set up experimental developer branches, see [TH03].)

Sometimes the real world is not so willing, and it might take a few hours or even a few days to work out all of the incompatible bits and pieces, during which time the build is broken. If it can't be helped, then make sure that it is well-communicated. Make sure everyone knows that the build will be broken for the requisite amount of time so that everyone can plan around it as needed. If you're not involved, maybe it would be a good time to take your car in for an oil change or slip off to the beach for a day or two. If you are involved, get it done quickly so everyone else can come back from the beach and get to work!

8.3 Test Frequency

How often should you run unit tests? It depends on what you're doing, and your personal habits, but here are some general guidelines that we find helpful. You want to perform enough testing to make sure you're catching everything you need to catch, but not so much testing that it interferes with producing production code.

Write a new method
    Compile and run local unit tests.

Fix a bug

Run tests to demonstrate bug; fix and re-run unit tests.

Any successful compile

Run local unit tests.

Each check-in to version control

Run all module or system unit tests.

Continuously

A dedicated machine should be running a full build and test, from scratch, automatically throughout the day (either periodically or on check-in to version control).

Note that for larger projects, you might not be able to compile and test the whole system in under a few hours. You may only be able to run a full build and test overnight. For even larger projects, it may have to be every couple of days—and that's a shame, because the longer the time between automatic builds the longer the "feedback gap" between creation of a problem and it's identification.

The reason to have a more-or-less continuous build is so that it can identify any problems quickly. You don't want to have to wait for another developer to stumble upon a build problem if you can help it. Having a build machine act as a constant developer increases the odds that *it* will find a problem, instead of a real developer.

When the build machine does find a problem, then the whole team can be alerted to the fact that it's not safe to get any new code just yet, and can continue working with what they have. That's better than getting stuck in a situation where you've gotten fresh code that doesn't work.

For more information on setting up automatic build and testing systems, nightly and continuous builds, and automation in general please see [Cla04].

8.4 Tests and Legacy Code

So far, we've talked about performing unit tests in the context of new code. But we haven't said what to do if your project has a lot of code already—code that *doesn't* have unit tests.

It all depends on what kind of state that code is in. If it's reasonably well-factored and modular, such that you can get at all of the individual pieces you need to, then you can add unit tests fairly easily. If, on the other hand, it's just a "big ball of mud" all tangled together, then it might be close to impossible to test without substantial rewriting. Most older projects aren't perfectly factored, but are usually modular enough that you can add unit tests.

For new code that you write, you'll obviously write unit tests as well. This may mean that you'll have to expose or break out parts of the existing system, or create mock objects in order to test your new functionality.

For existing code, you might choose to methodically add unit tests for everything that is testable. But that's not very pragmatic. It's better to add tests for the most broken stuff first, to realize a better return on investment of effort.

The most important aspect of unit tests in this environment is to prevent back-sliding: to avoid the death-spiral where maintenance fixes and enhancements cause bugs in existing features. We use NUnit unit tests as *regression* tests during normal new code development (to make sure new code doesn't break anything that had been working), but regression testing is even more important when dealing with legacy code.

And it doesn't have to cover the entire legacy code base, just the painful parts. Consider the following true story from a pragmatic developer (the team in question happened to be using Java and JUnit for this particular project, but they could just as easily have been using C#, Cobol, C++, Ruby, or any other programming language):

Regression Tests Save the Day

"Tibbert Enterprises[1] ships multiple applications, all of which are based on a common Lower Level Library that is used to access the object database.

One day I overheard some application developers talking about a persistent problem they were

---

[1]Not their real name.

having. In the product's Lower Level interface, you can look up objects using the object name, which includes a path to the object. Since the application has several layers between it and the Lower Level code, and the Lower Level code has several more layers to reach the object database, it takes a while to isolate a problem when the application breaks.

And the application broke. After half the application team spent an entire day tracking down the bug, they discovered the bug was in the Lower Level code that accessed the database. If you had a space in the name, the application died a violent, messy death. After isolating the Lower Level code related to the database access, they presented the bug to the owner of the code, along with a fix. He thanked them, incorporated their fix, and committed the fixed code into the repository.

But the next day, the application died. Once again, a team of application developers tracked it down. It took only a half-a-day this time (as they recognized the code paths by now), and the bug was in the same place. This time, it was a space in the path to the object that was failing, instead of a space in the name itself. Apparently, while integrating the fix, the developer had introduced a new bug. Once again, they tracked it down and presented him with a fix. It's Day Three, and the application is failing again! Apparently the developer in question re-introduced the original bug.

The application manager and I sat down and figured out that the equivalent of nearly two man-months of effort had been spent on this one issue over the course of one week by his team alone (and this likely affected other teams throughout the company). We then developed JUnit tests that tested the Lower Level API calls that the application product was using, and added tests for database access using spaces in both the object name and in the path. We put the product under the control of our continuous-build-and-test program (using Cruise-Control) so that the unit tests were run automatically every time code got committed back to the repository.

Sure enough, the following week, the test failed on two successive days, at the hands of the original developer. He actually came to my office, shook my hand, and thanked me when he got the automatic notification that the tests had failed.

You see, without the JUnit test, the bad code made it out to the entire company during the nightly builds. But with our continuous build and test, he (and his manager and tester) saw the failure at once, and he was able to fix it immediately before anyone else in the company used the code. In fact, this test has failed half a dozen times since then. But it gets caught, so its not a big deal anymore. The product is now stable because of these tests.

We now have a rule that any issue that pops up twice must have a JUnit test by the end of the week."

In this story, Tibbert Enterprises aren't using unit testing to prove things work so much as they are using it to inoculate against known issues. As they slowly catch up, they'll eventually expand to cover the entire product with unit tests, not just the most broken parts.

When you come into a shop with no automated tests of any kind, this seems to be a very effective approach. Remember, the only way to eat an elephant is one bite at a time.

8.5 Tests and Reviews

Teams that enjoy success often hold code reviews. This can be an informal affair where a senior person just gives a quick look at the code. Or perhaps two people are working on the code together, using Extreme Programming's "Pair Programming" practice. Or maybe it's a very formal affair with checklists and a small committee.

However you perform code reviews (and we suggest that you do), make the test code an integral part of the review process.

Since test code is held up to the same high standards as production code, it should be reviewed as well.

In fact, it can sometimes be helpful to expand on the idea of "test-first design" to include both writing and *reviewing* test code before writing production code. That is, code and review in this order:

1. Write test cases and/or test code.

2. Review test cases and/or test code.

3. Revise test cases and/or test code per review.

4. Write production code that passes the tests.

5. Review production and test code.

6. Revise test and production code per review.

Reviews of the test code are incredibly useful. Not only are reviews more effective than testing at finding bugs in the first place, but by having everyone involved in reviews you can improve team communication. People on the team get to see how others do testing, see what the team's conventions are, and help keep everyone honest.

You can use the checklists on page 145 of this book to help identify possible test cases in reviews. But don't go overboard testing things that aren't likely to break, or repeat essentially similar tests over and over just for the sake of testing.

Finally, you may want to keep track of common problems that come up again and again. These might be areas where more training might be needed, or perhaps something else that should be added to your standard review checklist.

For example, at a client's site several years ago, we discovered that many of the developers misunderstood exception handling. The code base was full of fragments similar to the following:

```
try {
    DatabaseConnection dbc = new DatabaseConnection();
    InsertNewRecord(dbc, record);
    dbc.Close();
} catch (Exception) {}
```

That is to say, they simply ignored any exceptions that might have occurred. Not only did this result in random missing records, but the system leaked database connections as well—any error that came up would cause the `Close` to be skipped.

We added this to the list of known, typical problems to be checked during reviews. As code was reviewed, any of these infamous `catch` statements that were discovered were first identified, then proper unit tests were put in place to force various error conditions (the "E" in RIGHT-BICEP), and the code was fixed to either propagate or handle the exception. System stability increased tremendously as a result of this simple process.

Chapter 9

Design Issues

So far we have discussed unit testing as it helps you to understand and verify the functional, operational characteristics of your code. But unit testing offers several opportunities to improve the design and architecture of your code as well.

In this chapter, we'll take a look at the following design-level issues:

- Better separation of concerns by designing for testability
- Clarifying design by defining class invariants
- Improving interfaces with test-driven design
- Establishing and localizing validation responsibilities

9.1 Designing for Testability

"Separation of Concerns" is probably the single most important concept in software design and implementation. It's the catch-all phrase that encompasses encapsulation, orthogonality, coupling, and all those other computer science terms that boil down to "write shy code" [HT00].

You can keep your code well-factored (i.e., "shy") and easier to maintain by explicitly designing code to be testable. For example, suppose you are writing a method that will sleep until the top of the next hour. You've got a bunch of calculations and then a `Sleep()`:

```
public void SleepUntilNextHour() {
    int howlong;
    XX XX.XX X XXX.X XX XX XXX,
    // Calculate how long to wait...
    X X XX XXX XXX X X XX;
    XX XX.XX X XXX.X XX XX XXX,

    Thread.Sleep(howlong);
    return;
}
```

How will you test that? Wait around for an hour? Set a timer, call the method, wait for the method to return, check the timer, handle the cases when the method doesn't get called when it should—this is starting to get pretty messy. We saw something similar back in Chapter 6, but this issue is important enough to revisit. Once again, we'll refactor the method in order to make testing easier.

Instead of combining the calculation of how many milliseconds to sleep with the Sleep() method itself, split them up:

```
public void SleepUntilNextHour() {
    int howlong = MilliSecondsToNextHour(DateTime.Now);
    Thread.Sleep(howlong);
    return;
}
```

What's likely to break? The system's Sleep call? Or our code that calculates the amount of time to wait? It's probably a fair bet to say that C#'s Thread.Sleep() works as advertised (even if it doesn't, our rule is to always suspect our own code first). So for now, you only need to test that the number of milliseconds is calculated correctly, and what might have been a hairy test with timers and all sorts of logic (not to mention an hour's wait) can be expressed very simply as:

```
Assert.AreEqual(10000, MilliSecondsToNextHour(DATE_1));
```

If we're confident that MilliSecondsToNextHour() works to our satisfaction, then the odds are that SleepUntilNextHour() will be reliable as well—if it is not, then at least we know that the problem must be related to the sleep itself, and not to the numerical calculation. You might even be able to reuse the MilliSecondsToNextHour() method in some other context.

This is what we mean when we claim that you can improve the design of code by making it easier to test. By changing code so that you can get in there and test it, you'll end up

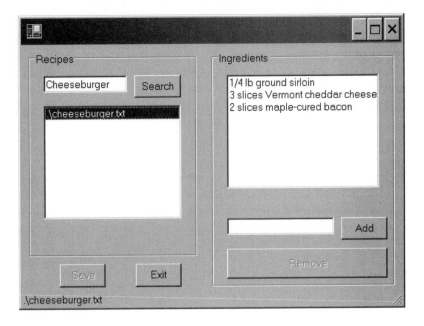

Figure 9.1: RECIPES GUI SCREEN

with a cleaner design that's easier to extend and maintain as well as test.

But instead of boring you with examples and techniques, all you really need to do is remember this one fundamental question when writing code:

How am I going to test this?

If the answer is not obvious, or if it looks like the test would be ugly or hard to write, then take that as a warning signal. Your design probably needs to be modified; change things around until the code is easy to test, and your design will end up being far better for the effort.

9.2 Refactoring for Testing

Let's look at a real-life example. Here are excerpts from a novice's first attempt at a recipe management system. The GUI, shown in Figure 9.1, is pretty straightforward. There's only one class, with GUI behavior and file I/O intermixed.

Figure 9.2: ORIGINAL RECIPES STATIC CLASS DIAGRAM

It reads and writes individual recipes to files, using a line-oriented format, somewhat like an INI or properties file:

```
NAME=Cheeseburger
INGREDIENTS=3
1/4 lb ground sirloin
3 slices Vermont cheddar cheese
2 slices maple-cured bacon
```

And here's the code, in it's entirety. As is, this is pretty hard to test. You've got to run the whole program and operate the GUI to get at any part of it. All of the file I/O and search routines access the widgets directly, and so are tightly coupled to the GUI code (see, for instance, lines 138, 150, 157, and 166). In fact, the UML diagram for this class, shown in Figure 9.2, is kind of embarrassing—it's just one big class!

```
Line 1  using System;
   -    using System.Drawing;
   -    using System.Collections;
   -    using System.ComponentModel;
   5    using System.Windows.Forms;
   -    using System.Data;
   -    using System.IO;
   -
   -    public class Recipes : Form {
   10     private Button exitButton = new Button();
   -       private StatusBar statusBar = new StatusBar();
   -       private GroupBox groupBox1 = new GroupBox();
   -       private TextBox titleText = new TextBox();
   -       private Button searchButton = new Button();
   15      private ListBox searchList = new ListBox();
   -       private GroupBox groupBox2 = new GroupBox();
   -       private ListBox ingredientsList = new ListBox();
   -       private Button removeButton = new Button();
   -       private TextBox ingredientsText = new TextBox();
   20      private Button saveButton = new Button();
   -       private Button addButton = new Button();
   -
```

```
        public Recipes() {
          InitializeComponent();
25      }

        private void InitializeComponent() {
          exitButton.Location =
            new System.Drawing.Point(120, 232);
30        exitButton.Size = new System.Drawing.Size(48, 24);
          exitButton.Text = "Exit";
          exitButton.Click +=
            new System.EventHandler(exitButton_Click);

35        statusBar.Location = new System.Drawing.Point(0, 261);
          statusBar.Size = new System.Drawing.Size(400, 16);

          groupBox1.Controls.Add(searchList);
          groupBox1.Controls.Add(searchButton);
40        groupBox1.Controls.Add(titleText);
          groupBox1.Location = new System.Drawing.Point(8, 8);
          groupBox1.Size = new System.Drawing.Size(176, 216);
          groupBox1.TabStop = false;
          groupBox1.Text = "Recipes";
45
          searchList.Location = new System.Drawing.Point(16, 56);
          searchList.Size = new System.Drawing.Size(144, 147);
          searchList.SelectedIndexChanged +=
            new System.EventHandler(
50            searchList_SelectedIndexChanged);

          searchButton.Location = new System.Drawing.Point(112, 24);
          searchButton.Size = new System.Drawing.Size(48, 24);
          searchButton.Text = "Search";
55        searchButton.Click +=
            new System.EventHandler(searchButton_Click);

          titleText.Location = new System.Drawing.Point(16, 24);
          titleText.Size = new System.Drawing.Size(88, 20);
60
          groupBox2.Controls.Add(addButton);
          groupBox2.Controls.Add(ingredientsText);
          groupBox2.Controls.Add(removeButton);
          groupBox2.Controls.Add(ingredientsList);
65        groupBox2.Location = new System.Drawing.Point(200, 8);
          groupBox2.Size = new System.Drawing.Size(192, 248);
          groupBox2.TabStop = false;
          groupBox2.Text = "Ingredients";

70        addButton.Location = new System.Drawing.Point(136, 176);
          addButton.Size = new System.Drawing.Size(48, 23);
          addButton.Text = "Add";
          addButton.Click +=
            new System.EventHandler(addButton_Click);
75
          ingredientsText.Location = new System.Drawing.Point(16, 176);
          ingredientsText.Size = new System.Drawing.Size(112, 20);

          removeButton.Enabled = false;
80        removeButton.Location = new System.Drawing.Point(16, 208);
          removeButton.Size = new System.Drawing.Size(168, 32);
          removeButton.Text = "Remove";
          removeButton.Click +=
            new System.EventHandler(removeButton_Click);
85
```

```
     ingredientsList.Location = new System.Drawing.Point(16, 24);
     ingredientsList.Size = new System.Drawing.Size(160, 134);
     ingredientsList.SelectedIndexChanged +=
       new System.EventHandler(
90       ingredientsList_SelectedIndexChanged);

     saveButton.Enabled = false;
     saveButton.Location = new System.Drawing.Point(40, 232);
     saveButton.Size = new System.Drawing.Size(48, 24);
95   saveButton.Text = "Save";
     saveButton.Click +=
       new System.EventHandler(saveButton_Click);

     AutoScaleBaseSize = new System.Drawing.Size(5, 13);
100  ClientSize = new System.Drawing.Size(400, 277);
     Controls.Add(saveButton);
     Controls.Add(groupBox2);
     Controls.Add(groupBox1);
     Controls.Add(statusBar);
105  Controls.Add(exitButton);
     groupBox1.ResumeLayout(false);
     groupBox2.ResumeLayout(false);
     ResumeLayout(false);
   }
110
   [STAThread]
   static void Main() {
     Directory.SetCurrentDirectory(@"..\..\recipes\");
     Application.Run(new Recipes());
115  }

   private void exitButton_Click(object sender,
                                 System.EventArgs e) {
     Application.Exit();
120  }

   private void searchButton_Click(object sender,
                                   System.EventArgs e) {
     String toMatch = "*" + titleText.Text + "*";
125
     try {
       string [] matchingFiles = Directory.GetFiles(@".", toMatch);
       searchList.DataSource = matchingFiles;
     }
130  catch (Exception error) {
       statusBar.Text = error.Message;
     }
   }
135  private void
   searchList_SelectedIndexChanged(object sender,
                                   System.EventArgs e) {
     string file = (string)searchList.SelectedItem;
     string line;
140  char [] delim = new char[] { '=' };

     statusBar.Text = file;

     using (StreamReader reader =
145            new StreamReader(file)) {
```

```
  -         while ((line = reader.ReadLine()) != null) {
  -           string [] parts = line.Split(delim, 2);
  -           switch (parts[0]) {
  -             case "NAME":
150               titleText.Text = parts[1];
  -               break;
  -             case "INGREDIENTS":
  -               try {
  -                 int count = Int32.Parse(parts[1]);
155               ingredientsList.Items.Clear();
  -                 for (int i = 0; i < count; i++)
  -                   ingredientsList.Items.Add(reader.ReadLine());
  -               }
  -               catch (Exception error) {
160               statusBar.Text = "Bad ingredient count: " +
  -                   error.Message;
  -                 return;
  -               }
  -               break;
165           default:
  -               statusBar.Text = "Invalid recipe line: " + line;
  -               return;
  -           }
  -         }
170       }
  -       saveButton.Enabled = false;
  -     }
  -
  -     private void removeButton_Click(object sender,
175                                    System.EventArgs e) {
  -       int index = ingredientsList.SelectedIndex;
  -       if (index >= 0) {
  -         statusBar.Text = "Removed " +
  -           ingredientsList.SelectedItem;
180       ingredientsList.Items.RemoveAt(index);
  -         saveButton.Enabled = true;
  -       }
  -     }
  -
185     private void addButton_Click(object sender,
  -                                  System.EventArgs e) {
  -       string newIngredient = ingredientsText.Text;
  -       if (newIngredient.Length > 0) {
  -         ingredientsList.Items.Add(newIngredient);
190       saveButton.Enabled = true;
  -       }
  -     }
  -
  -     private void
195     ingredientsList_SelectedIndexChanged(object sender,
  -                                          System.EventArgs e) {
  -       int index = ingredientsList.SelectedIndex;
  -       if (index < 0)
  -         removeButton.Enabled = false;
200     else {
  -         removeButton.Text = "Remove " +
  -           ingredientsList.SelectedItem;
  -         removeButton.Enabled = true;
  -       }
```

```
205       }

          private void saveButton_Click(object sender,
                                          System.EventArgs e) {
            string fileName = titleText.Text + ".txt";
210         ICollection items = ingredientsList.Items;
            using (StreamWriter file =
                        new StreamWriter(fileName, false)) {
              file.WriteLine("NAME={0}", titleText.Text);
              file.WriteLine("INGREDIENTS={0}", items.Count);
215           foreach (string line in items) {
                file.WriteLine(line);
              }
            }
            statusBar.Text = "Saved " + fileName;
220       }
        }
```

We clearly need to improve this code. Let's begin by making a separate object to hold a recipe, so that we can construct test recipe data easily and toss it back and forth to the screen, disk, network, or wherever. This is just a simple data holder, with accessors for the data members.

```
Line 1  using System;
        using System.Collections;

        public class Recipe : IEnumerable {
5         protected String name;
          protected ArrayList ingredients;

          public Recipe() {
            name = "";
10          ingredients = new ArrayList();
          }

          public Recipe(Recipe another) {
            name = another.name;
15          ingredients = new ArrayList(another.ingredients);
          }

          public String Name {
            get { return name; }
20          set { name = value; }
          }

          public void AddIngredient(String aThing) {
            ingredients.Add(aThing);
25        }

          public IEnumerator GetEnumerator() {
            return ingredients.GetEnumerator();
          }
30        public int NumIngredients {
            get { return ingredients.Count; }
          }
        }
```

Next, we need to pull the code out from the original `Recipes` class to save and load a file to disk.

To help separate file I/O from any other kind of I/O, we'll perform the file I/O in a helper class that uses `Recipe`. We want to take out all of the GUI widget references from the original source code, and use instance member variables instead.

```
Line 1    public class RecipeFile {

            public Recipe Load(String fileName) {
              Recipe result = new Recipe();
      5       string line;
              char [] delim = new char[] { '=' };

              using (StreamReader reader = new StreamReader(fileName)) {
                while ((line = reader.ReadLine()) != null) {
     10           string [] parts = line.Split(delim, 2);
                  switch (parts[0]) {
                    case "TITLE":
                      result.Name = parts[1];
                      break;
     15             case "INGREDIENTS":
                      try {
                        int count = Int32.Parse(parts[1]);
                        for (int i = 0; i < count; i++)
                          result.AddIngredient(reader.ReadLine());
     20               } catch (Exception error) {
                        throw new RecipeFormatException(
                          "Bad ingredient count: " + error.Message);
                      }
                      break;
     25           }
                }
              }
              return result;
            }
     30
            public void Save(String fileName, Recipe recipe)  {
              using (StreamWriter file =
                      new StreamWriter(fileName, false)) {
                file.WriteLine("NAME={0}", recipe.Name);
     35         file.WriteLine("INGREDIENTS={0}",
                  recipe.NumIngredients);
                foreach (String line in recipe) {
                  file.WriteLine(line);
                }
     40       }
            }
          }
```

RecipeFile.cs

Now we're in a position where we can write a genuine test case that will test reading and writing to disk, without using any GUI code.

```
Line 1   using System;
    -    using System.Collections;
    -    using System.IO;
    -    using NUnit.Framework;
    5
    -    [TestFixture]
    -    public class TestRecipe {

    -      [Test]
   10      public void SaveandRestore() {

    -        const String test_name =
    -                "Cheeseburger";
    -        const String test_ing1 =
   15               "1/4 lb ground sirloin";
    -        const String test_ing2 =
    -                "3 slices Vermont cheddar cheese";
    -        const String test_ing3 =
    -                "2 slices maple-cured bacon";
   20
    -        // Save one out
    -        Recipe rec = new Recipe();
    -        rec.Name = test_name;
    -        rec.AddIngredient(test_ing1);
   25        rec.AddIngredient(test_ing2);
    -        rec.AddIngredient(test_ing3);

    -        RecipeFile filer = new RecipeFile();
    -        filer.Save("test.recipe", rec);
   30
    -        try {
    -          // Now get it back
    -          Recipe rec2 = new Recipe();
    -          filer = new RecipeFile();
   35          rec2 = filer.Load("test.recipe");

    -          Assert.AreEqual(test_name, rec2.Name);
    -          IEnumerator itr = rec2.GetEnumerator();

   40          Assert.AreEqual(test_ing1, itr.Current);
    -          itr.MoveNext();
    -          Assert.AreEqual(test_ing2, itr.Current);
    -          itr.MoveNext();
    -          Assert.AreEqual(test_ing3, itr.Current);
   45          itr.MoveNext();
    -          Assert.IsFalse(itr.MoveNext());
    -        } finally {
    -          File.Delete("test.recipe");
    -        }
   50      }
    -    }
```

TestRecipe.cs

At line 13 we'll declare some constant strings for testing. Then we make a new, empty object and populate it with the test data beginning at line 23. We could just pass literal strings directly into the object instead, and not bother with const data members, but since we'll need to check the results against these strings, it makes sense to put them in common constants that we can reference from both spots.

With a `Recipe` data object now fully populated, we'll call the `Save()` method to write the recipe to disk at line 29. Now we can make a brand-new `Recipe` object, and ask the helper to load it from that same file at line 35.

With the restored object in hand, we can now proceed to run a whole bunch of asserts to make sure that the test data we set in the `rec` object has been restored in the `rec2` object.

Finally, at line 48 we play the part of a good neighbor and delete the temporary file we used for the test. Note that we use a `finally` clause to ensure that the file gets deleted, even if one of our assertions fails.

Now we can run the unit test in the usual fashion to make sure that the code is reading and writing to disk okay.

Try running this example before reading on...

```
Failures:
1) TestRecipe.SaveandRestore :
   String lengths differ.  Expected length=12, but was length=0.
   Strings differ at index 0.

   expected:<"Cheeseburger">
   but was:<"">
   ---------^
   at TestRecipe.SaveandRestore() in testrecipe.cs:line 37
```

Whoops! Seems that wasn't working as well as we thought— we're not getting the name line of the recipe back. When we save the file out in `RecipeFile.cs`, the code is using the key string `"NAME"` to identify the field, but when we read it back in (line 12 of `Load()`), it's trying to use the string `"TITLE"`. That's just not going to work. We can easily change that to read `"NAME"`, to match the key used for the save, but stop and ask yourself the critical question:

Could this happen anywhere else in the code?

Using strings as keys is a fine idea, but it does open the door to introduce errors due to misspellings or inconsistent naming as we've seen here. So perhaps this failing test is trying to tell you something more—perhaps you should refactor the code and pull out those literal strings into constants. The class then looks like this:

```
Line 1    public class RecipeFile {

            const String NAME_TOK = "NAME";
            const String INGREDIENTS_TOK = "INGREDIENTS";
    5
            public Recipe Load(String fileName) {
              Recipe result = new Recipe();
              string line;
              char [] delim = new char[] { '=' };
    10
              using (StreamReader reader = new StreamReader(fileName)) {
                while ((line = reader.ReadLine()) != null) {
                  string [] parts = line.Split(delim, 2);
                  switch (parts[0]) {
    15                case NAME_TOK:
                        result.Name = parts[1];
                        break;
                      case INGREDIENTS_TOK:
                        try {
    20                      int count = Int32.Parse(parts[1]);
                          for (int i = 0; i < count; i++)
                            result.AddIngredient(reader.ReadLine());
                        } catch (Exception error) {
                          throw new RecipeFormatException(
    25                        "Bad ingredient count: " + error.Message);
                        }
                        break;
                  }
                }
    30        }
              return result;
            }

            public void Save(String fileName, Recipe recipe)  {
    35        using (StreamWriter file =
                    new StreamWriter(fileName, false)) {
                file.WriteLine("{0}={1}",
                  NAME_TOK, recipe.Name);
                file.WriteLine("{0}={1}",
    40            INGREDIENTS_TOK, recipe.NumIngredients);
                foreach (String line in recipe) {
                  file.WriteLine(line);
                }
              }
    45      }
          }
```

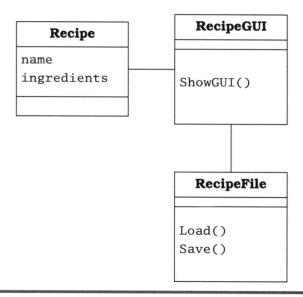

Figure 9.3: REFACTORED RECIPES STATIC CLASS DIAGRAM

We've improved the original program a lot with these simple changes. In order to test the file I/O, we:

- Made Recipe a first-class object

- Moved file I/O routines out of the GUI and into Recipe-File

- Pulled literals into constants to avoid bugs from typos

Finally, now that we have unit tests that provide the basic capabilities of a Recipe, we need to re-integrate the new Recipe class into the GUI itself and tend to the file I/O. We'd like to end up with something like Figure 9.3.

Now RecipeGUI holds an object of type Recipe, and uses the helper class RecipeFile to read and write recipes to disk. When the user presses the save button, the GUI will set values from the widgets in the Recipe object and call RecipeFile.Save(). When a new recipe is loaded in, the GUI will get the proper values from the Recipe object returned from RecipeFile.Load().

Testing GUI's is hard, and isn't always worth the extreme effort. By separating the pure GUI from the guts of the application, you can easily add and test business features without involving the GUI.

The main GUI class `RecipeGUI` (formerly known as `Recipes`) should now contain nothing but GUI-oriented code: widgets, callbacks, and so on. Thus, all of the "business logic" and file I/O can be in non-GUI, fully testable classes.

And we've got a clean design as an added bonus.

9.3 Testing the Class Invariant

Another way to improve the design of a class is by defining and verifying the "class invariant."[1]

A class invariant is an assertion, or some set of assertions, about objects of a class. For an object to be valid, all of these assertions must be true. They cannot vary.

For instance, a class that implements a sorted list may have the invariant that its contents are in sorted order. That means that no matter what else happens, no matter what methods are called, the list must always be in sorted order—at least as viewed from outside the object. Within a method, of course, the invariant may be momentarily violated as the class performs whatever housekeeping is necessary. But by the time the method returns, or the object is otherwise available for use (as in a multi-threaded environment), the invariant must hold true or else it indicates a bug.

That means it's something you could check for as part of every unit test for this class.

The invariant is generally an artifact of implementation: internal counters, the fact that certain member variables are populated, and so on. The invariant is not the place to check for user input validation or anything of that sort. When writing tests, you want to test just your one thing, but at the same time you want to make sure the overall state of the class is consistent—you want to make sure you have not inflicted any collateral damage.

---

[1] For more information on pre-conditions, post-conditions and invariants, see [Mey97].

Here are some possible areas where class invariants might apply.

Structural

The most common invariants are structural in nature. That is, they refer to structural properties of data. For instance, in an order-entry system you might have invariants such as:

- Every line item must belong to an order

- Every order must have one or more line items

When working with arrays of data, you'll typically maintain a member variable that acts as an index into the array. The invariants on that index would include:

- index must be $>= 0$

- index must be $<$ array length

You want to check the invariant if any of these conditions are likely to break. Suppose you are performing some sort of calculation on the index into an array; you'd want to check the invariant throughout your unit tests to make sure the class is never in an inconsistent state. We showed this in the stack class example on page 60.

Structural errors will usually cause the program to throw an exception and/or terminate abruptly. For that matter, so will failing the invariant check. The difference is that when the invariant is violated, you know about it right away—right at the scene of the crime. You'll probably also know exactly what condition was violated. Without the invariant, the failure may occur far from the original bug, and backtracking to the cause might take you anywhere from a few minutes to a few *days*.

More importantly, checking the invariant makes sure that you aren't passing the tests based just on luck. It may be that there's a bug that the tests aren't catching that will blow up under real conditions. The invariant might help you catch that early, even if an explicit test does not.

Mathematical

Other constraints are more mathematical in nature. Instead of verifying the physical nature of data structures, you may need to consider the logical model. For example:

- Debits and credits on a bank account match the balance.

- Amounts measured in different units match after conversion (an especially popular issue with spacecraft).

This starts to sound a lot like the boundary conditions we discussed earlier, and in a way they are. The difference is that an invariant must always be true for the entire visible state of a class. It's not just a fleeting condition; it's *always* true.

Data Consistency

Often times an object may present the same data in different ways—a list of items in a shopping cart, the total amount of the sale, and the total number of items in the cart are closely related. From a list of items with details, you can derive the other two figures. It must be an invariant that these figures are consistent. If not, then there's a bug.

9.4 Test-Driven Design

Test-driven development is a valuable technique where you always write the tests themselves *before* writing the methods that they test [Bec00]. As a nice side benefit of this style of working, you can enjoy "test-driven design" and significantly improve the design of your interfaces.

You'll get better interfaces (or API's) because you are "eating your own dog food," as the saying goes—you are able to apply feedback to improve the design.

That is, by writing the tests first, you have now placed yourself in the role of a *user* of your code, instead of the *implementor* of your code. From this perspective, you can usually get a much better sense of how an interface will really be used, and might see opportunities to improve its design.

For example, suppose you're writing a routine that does some special formatting for printed pages. There are a bunch of dimensions that need to be specified, so you code up the first version like this:

```
AddCropMarks(PSStream str, double paper_width,
                        double paper_height,
                        double body_width,
                        double body_height);
```

Then as you start to write the tests (based on real-world data) you notice that a pattern emerges from the test code:

```
public Process() {
    xxx xx xxxx xx x xx xxx xx xxx xx xx;
    x xx x xxx xxx xx xx xx xxxx xxxx
    AddCropMarks(str, 8.5, 11.0, 6.0, 8.5);
    xx xxx x xxx xx xx x xxx xxx xxx xx xx xxx;
    x xxx xxx xxxx x xxx xxx xxx xxx xx xx;
    AddCropMarks(str, 8.5, 11.0, 6.0, 8.5);
    xx xx xxx xx xx xxx xxx xxx xxxx xx xx xx xx;
    x xx xx x xxxx xxx x xxxx xx xx xx xx xxx xx;
    AddCropMarks(str, 8.5, 11.0, 6.0, 8.5);
    xxx xx xxxxxx xxx xxx xxxx x xxx xxxx xx xxxxx;
    xx x xxx xxxx xxxx xxx xxxx xxxx xx x x xx xx;
    AddCropMarks(str, 5.0, 7.0, 4.0, 5.5);
    xx xxx xx xx x xxxx xxx xx x xxx xxxx xx xxx xx;
    xxx xx xxxx xx xx xxx x xxx xxxx xx xx xx xxx;
    AddCropMarks(str, 5.0, 7.0, 4.0, 5.5);
    xx xx xxxxx xx x xx xxx xx xxxx xx xx;
    x xxx x xxx xxx xx xx xxx xxxx xx;

}
```

As it turns out, there are only a handful of common paper sizes in use, but you still need to allow for odd-ball sizes as necessary. So the first thing to do—just to make the tests easier, of course—is to factor out the size specification into a separate object.

```
PaperSpec standardPaper1 = new PaperSpec(8.5, 11.0,
                                         6.0, 8.5);
PaperSpec standardPaper2 = new PaperSpec(5.0, 7.0,
                                         4.0, 5.5);
xxx xx xxxxxx xxx xxx xxxx x xxx xxxx xx xxxxx,
xx x xxx xxxx xxxx xxx xxxx xxxx xx x x xx xx;
AddCropMarks(str, standardPaper1);
AddCropMarks(str, standardPaper1);
xx xxx xx xx x xxx xxx xxx xxxx xx xx xx xxx xx;
xxx xx xxxxx xx xx xxx x xxx xxxx xx xx xx xxx;
AddCropMarks(str, standardPaper2);
```

Now the tests are much cleaner and easier to follow, and the application code that uses this will be cleaner as well.

Since these standard paper sizes don't vary, we can make a factory class that will encapsulate the creation of all the standard paper sizes.

```
public class StandardPaperFactory {
  public static PaperSpec LetterInstance;
  public static PaperSpec A4Instance;
  public static PaperSpec LegalInstance;
  ...
  ...
}
```

By making the tests cleaner and easier to write, you will make the real code cleaner and easier to write as well.

Try it

Exercises

Answer on 153

7. Design an interest calculator that calculates the amount of interest based on the number of working days in-between two dates. Use test-first design, and take it one step at a time.

9.5 Testing Invalid Parameters

One question that comes up when folks first start testing is: "Do I have to test whether my class validates it parameters?" The answer, in best consultant fashion, is "it depends...."

Is your class supposed to validate its parameters? If so, then yes, you need to test that this functionality is correct. But there's a larger question here: Who's responsible for validating input data?

In many systems, the answer is mixed, or haphazard at best. You can't really trust that any other part of the system has checked the input data, so you have to check it yourself—or at least, that aspect of the input data that particularly concerns you. In effect, the data ends up being checked by everyone and no one. Besides being a grotesque violation of the DRY principle [HT00], it wastes a lot of time and energy—and we typically don't have that much extra to waste.

In a well-designed system, you establish up-front the parts of the system that need to perform validation, and localize those to a small and well-known part of the system.

So the first question you should ask about a system is, "who is *supposed* to check the validity of input data?"

Generally we find the easiest rule to adopt is the "keep the barbarians out at the gate" approach. Check input at the boundaries of the system, and you won't have to duplicate those tests inside the system. Internal components can trust that if the data has made it this far into the system, then it must be okay.

It's sort of like a hospital operating room or industrial "clean room" approach. You undergo elaborate cleaning rituals before you—or any tools or materials—can enter the room, but once there you are assured of a sterile field. If the field becomes contaminated, it's a major catastrophe; you have to re-sterilize the whole environment.

Any part of the software system that is outward-facing (a UI, or interface to another system) needs to be robust, and not allow any incorrect or unvalidated data through. What defines "correct" or valid data should be part of specification you're testing against.

What does any of this have to do with unit testing?

It makes a difference with regard to what you need to test against. As we mentioned earlier, if it isn't your code's responsibility to check for input data problems, then don't waste time checking for it. If it *is* your responsibility, then you need to be extra vigilant—because now the rest of the system is potentially relying on you, and you alone.

But that's okay. You've got unit tests.

Gotchas

Here are some popular "gotchas," that is, issues, problems, or misconceptions that have popped up over and over again to trap the unwary.

A.1 As Long As The Code Works

Some folks seem to think that it's okay to live with broken unit tests as long as the code itself works. Code without tests— or code with broken tests—*is* broken. You just don't know where, or when. In this case, you've really got the worst of both worlds: all that effort writing tests in the first place is wasted, and you still have no confidence that the code is doing what it ought.

If the tests are broken, treat it just as if the code were broken.

A.2 "Smoke" Tests

Some developers believe that a "smoke test" is good enough for unit testing. That is, if a method makes it all the way to the end without blowing up, then it passed.

You can readily identify this sort of a test: there are no asserts within the test itself, just one big `Assert.IsTrue(true)` at the end. Maybe the slightly more adventurous will have multiple `Assert.IsTrue(true)`'s throughout, but no more than that. All they are testing is, "did it make it this far?"

And that's just not enough. Without validating any data or other behavior, all you're doing is lulling yourself into a false sense of security—you might think the code is tested, but it is not.

Watch out for this style of testing, and correct it as soon as possible. **Real testing checks results.** Anything else is just wasting everyone's time.

A.3 "Works On My Machine"

Another pathologic problem that turns up on some projects is that old excuse, "It's not broken, it works on my machine." This points to a bug that has some correlation with the environment. When this happens, ask yourself:

- Is everything under version control?

- Is the development environment consistent on the affected machines?

- Is it a genuine bug that just happens to manifest itself on another machine (because it's faster, or has more or less memory, etc.)?

End users, in particular, don't like to hear that the code works on *your* machine and not theirs.

All tests must pass on *all* machines; otherwise the code is broken.

A.4 Floating-Point Problems

Quite a few developers appear to have missed that one day in class when they talked about floating-point numbers. It's a fact of life that there are floating point numbers that can only be approximately represented in computer hardware. The computer only has so many bits to work with, so something has to give.

This means that `1.333` + `1.333` isn't going to equal `2.666` exactly. It will be close, but not exact. That's why the NUnit floating-point asserts require you to specify a *tolerance* along with the desired values (see the discussion on page 29).

But still you need to be aware that "close enough" may be deceptive at times. Your tests may be too lenient for the real world's requirements, for instance. Or you might puzzle at an error message that says:

```
Failures:
1) TestXyz.TestMe :
        expected:<1.00000000>
          but was:<1.00000000>
   at TestXyz.TestMe() in TestXyz.cs:line 10
```

"Gosh, they sure look equal to me!" But they aren't—there must a difference that's smaller than is being displayed by the print method.

As a side note, you can get a similar problem when using date and time types. Two dates might look equal as they are normally displayed—but maybe the milliseconds aren't equal.

A.5 Tests Take Too Long

Unit tests need to run fairly quickly. After all, you'll be running them a lot. But suddenly you might notice that the tests are taking *too long*. It's slowing you down as you write tests and code during the day.

That means it's time to go through and look at your tests with a fresh eye. Cull out individual tests that take longer than average to run, and group them together somewhere.

You can run these optional, longer-running tests once a day with the build, or when you check in, but not have to run them every single time you change code.

Just don't move them so far out of the way that they *never* get run.

A.6 Tests Keep Breaking

Some teams notice that the tests keep breaking over and over again. Small changes to the code base suddenly break tests all over the place, and it takes a remarkable amount of effort to get everything working again.

This is usually a sign of excessive coupling. Test code might be too tightly-coupled to external data, to other parts of the system, and so on.

As soon as you identify this as a problem, you need to fix it. Isolate the necessary parts of the system to make the tests more robust, using the same techniques you would use to minimize coupling in production code. See [HT00] for more details on orthogonality and coupling, or [FBB+99] for information on refactoring and design smells, and don't forget to use Mock Objects (Chapter 6) to decouple yourself from the real world.

A.7 Tests Fail on Some Machines

Here's a common nightmare scenario: all the tests run fine—on most machines. But on certain machines they fail consistently. Maybe on some machines they even fail intermittently.

What on earth could be going on? What could be different on these different machines?

The obvious answer is differences in the version of the operating system, libraries, the C# runtime engine, the database driver; that sort of thing. Different versions of software have different bugs, workarounds, and features, so it's quite possible that machines configured differently might behave differently.

But what if the machines are configured with identical software, and you still get different results?

It might be that one machine runs a little faster than the other, and the difference in timing reveals a race condition or other problem with concurrency. The same thing can show up on single vs. multiple-processor machines.

It's a real bug, it just happened not to have shown up before. Track it down on the affected machine using the usual methods. Prove the bug exists *on that machine* as best you can, and verify that all tests pass *on all machines* when you are done.

Appendix B

Resources

B.1 On The Web

Cruise Control .NET
⇒ http://ccnet.thoughtworks.com
CruiseControl.NET is an automated Continuous Integration server
for the Microsoft .NET platform that integrates with Nant, NUnit, and
most major open source and proprietary version control systems.

DotNetMock
⇒ http://sourceforge.net/projects/dotnetmock
A repository for Mock Object information in the .NET environment,
as well as testing in general.

NCover
⇒ http://workspaces.gotdotnet.com/ncover
A simple code coverage tool that runs from the command line and
outputs an XML file with the code coverage statistics. Requires
pdb files for monitored assemblies, and produces line-by-line visit
counts. Also includes a simple XSLT transform to make the output
readable in a browser.

NMock
⇒ http://nmock.truemesh.com
NMock is a dynamic mock-object library for .NET.

NUnit
⇒ http://nunit.org
This xUnit-based unit testing tool for Microsoft .NET is written entirely in C# and has been completely redesigned to take advantage
of many .NET language features, including custom attributes and

other reflection related capabilities. NUnit brings xUnit to all .NET languages.

NUnit-Addin
⇒ http://www.mutantdesign.co.uk/nunit-addin
Visual-Studio integration for NUnit.

Pragmatic Programming
⇒ http://www.pragmaticprogrammer.com
Home page for Pragmatic Programming and your authors. Here you'll find all of the source code examples from this book, additional resources, updated URLs and errata, and news on additional volumes in this series and other resources.

xUnit
⇒ http://www.xprogramming.com/software.htm
Unit testing frameworks for many, many different languages and environments.

B.2 Bibliography

[Bec00] Kent Beck. *Extreme Programming Explained: Embrace Change.* Addison-Wesley, Reading, MA, 2000.

[Cla04] Mike Clark. *Pragmatic Automation.* The Pragmatic Programmers, LLC, Raleigh, NC, and Dallas, TX, (planned for) 2004.

[FBB+99] Martin Fowler, Kent Beck, John Brant, William Opdyke, and Don Roberts. *Refactoring: Improving the Design of Existing Code.* Addison Wesley Longman, Reading, MA, 1999.

[HT00] Andrew Hunt and David Thomas. *The Pragmatic Programmer: From Journeyman to Master.* Addison-Wesley, Reading, MA, 2000.

[Mey97] Bertrand Meyer. *Object-Oriented Software Construction.* Prentice Hall, Englewood Cliffs, NJ, second edition, 1997.

[MFC01] Tim Mackinnon, Steve Freeman, and Philip Craig. Endo-testing: Unit testing with mock objects. In Giancarlo Succi and Michele Marchesi, editors, *Extreme Programming Examined*, chapter 17, pages 287–302. Addison Wesley Longman, Reading, MA, 2001.

[TH03] Dave Thomas and Andy Hunt. *Pragmatic Version Control.* The Pragmatic Programmers, LLC, Raleigh, NC, and Dallas, TX, 2003.

Pragmatic Unit Testing: Summary

General Principles:

☐ Test anything that might break

☐ Test everything that does break

☐ New code is guilty until proven innocent

☐ Write at least as much test code as production code

☐ Run local tests with each compile

☐ Run all tests before check-in to repository

Questions to Ask:

☐ If the code ran correctly, how would I know?

☐ How am I going to test this?

☐ What *else* can go wrong?

☐ Could this same kind of problem happen anywhere else?

What to Test: Use Your RIGHT-BICEP

☐ Are the results **right**?

☐ Are all the **boundary** conditions CORRECT?

☐ Can you check **inverse** relationships?

☐ Can you **cross-check** results using other means?

☐ Can you force **error conditions** to happen?

☐ Are **performance** characteristics within bounds?

Good tests are A TRIP

☐ **Automatic**

☐ **Thorough**

☐ **Repeatable**

☐ **Independent**

☐ **Professional**

CORRECT Boundary Conditions

☐ **Conformance** — Does the value conform to an expected format?

☐ **Ordering** — Is the set of values ordered or unordered as appropriate?

☐ **Range** — Is the value within reasonable minimum and maximum values?

☐ **Reference** — Does the code reference anything external that isn't under direct control of the code itself?

☐ **Existence** — Does the value exist? (e.g., is non-null, non-zero, present in a set, etc.)

☐ **Cardinality** — Are there exactly enough values?

☐ **Time** (absolute and relative) — Is everything happening in order? At the right time? In time?

Answers to Exercises

Exercise 1:   *from page 68*

A simple stack class. Push String objects onto the stack, and Pop them off according to normal stack semantics. This class provides the following methods:

```csharp
using System;

public interface StackExercise {

    /// <summary>
    /// Return and remove the most recent item from
    /// the top of the  stack.
    /// </summary>
    /// <exception cref="StackEmptyException">
    /// Throws exception if the stack is empty.
    /// </exception>
    String Pop();

    /// <summary>
    /// Add an item to the top of the stack.
    /// </summary>
    /// <param name="item">A String to push
    /// on the stack</param>
    void Push(String item);

    /// <summary>
    /// Return but do not remove the most recent
    /// item from the top of the stack.
    /// </summary>
    /// <exception cref="StackEmptyException">
    /// Throws exception if the stack is empty.
    /// </exception>
    String Top();

    /// <summary>
    /// Returns true if the stack is empty.
    /// </summary>
    bool IsEmpty();
}
```

Here are some hints to get you started: what is likely to break? How should the stack behave when it is first initialized? After it's been used for a while? Does it really do what it claims to do?

Answer 1:

- For a brand-new stack, `IsEmpty()` should be `true`, `Top()` and `Pop()` should throw exceptions.

- Starting with an empty stack, call `Push()` to push a test string onto the stack. Verify that `Top()` returns that string several times in a row, and that `IsEmpty()` returns `false`.

- Call `Pop()` to remove the test string, and verify that it is the same string.[1] `IsEmpty()` should now be `true`. Call `Pop()` again verify an exception is thrown.

- Now do the same test again, but this time add multiple items to the stack. Make sure you get the rights ones back, in the right order (the most recent item added should be the one returned).

- Push a `null` onto the stack and `Pop` it; confirm you get a `null` back.

- Ensure you can use the stack after it has thrown exceptions.

Exercise 2:   *from page 69*
A shopping cart. This class lets you add, delete, and count the items in a shopping cart.

What sort of boundary conditions might come up? Are there any implicit restrictions on what you can delete? Are there any interesting issues if the cart is empty?

```
public interface ShoppingCart {
    /// <summary>
    /// Add this many of this item to the
    /// shopping cart.
    /// </summary>
    /// <exception cref="NegativeCountException">
    /// </exception>
    void AddItems(Item anItem, int quantity);

    /// <summary>
    /// Delete this many of this item from the
    /// shopping cart
    /// </summary>
    /// <exception cref="NegativeCountException">
    /// </exception>
    /// <exception cref="NoSuchItemException">
```

---

[1]In this case, `Assert.AreEqual()` isn't good enough; you need `Assert.AreSame()` to ensure it's the same object.

```
/// </exception>
void DeleteItems(Item anItem, int quantity);

/// <summary>
/// Count of all items in the cart
/// (that is, all items x qty each)
/// </summary>
int ItemCount { get; }

/// Return iterator of all items
IEnumerable GetEnumerator();
}
```

ShoppingCart.cs

Answer 2:

- Call `AddItems` with quantity of 0 and `ItemCount` should remain the same.

- Call `DeleteItem` with quantity of 0 and `ItemCount` should remain the same.

- Call `AddItems` with a negative quantity and it should raise an exception.

- Call `DeleteItem` with a negative quantity and it should raise an exception.

- Call `AddItems` and the item count should increase, whether the item exists already or not.

- Call `DeleteItem` where the item doesn't exist and it should raise an exception.

- Call `DeleteItem` when there are no items in the cart and `ItemCount` should remain at 0.

- Call `DeleteItem` where the quantity is larger than the number of those items in the cart and it should raise an exception.

- Call `GetEnumerator` when there are no items in the cart and it should return an empty iterator (i.e., it's a real IEnumerable object (not null) that contains no items).

- Call `AddItem` several times for a couple of items and verify that contents of the cart match what was added (as reported via GetEnumerator() and ItemCount()).

Hint: you can combine several of these asserts into a single test. For instance, you might start with an empty cart, add 3 of an item, then delete one of them at a time.

Exercise 3: *from page 70*

A fax scheduler. This code will send faxes from a specified file name to a U.S. phone number. There is a validation requirement; a U.S. phone number with area code must be of the form *xnn-nnn-nnnn*, where *x* must be a digit in the range [2..9] and *n* can be [0..9]. The following blocks are reserved and are not currently valid area codes: *x*11, *x*9*n*, 37*n*, 96*n*.

The method's signature is:

```
///
/// Send the named file as a fax to the
/// given phone number.
/// <exception cref="MissingOrBadFileException">
/// </exception>
/// <exception cref="PhoneFormatException">
/// </exception>
/// <exception cref="PhoneAreaCodeException">
/// </exception>
public bool SendFax(String phone, String filename)
```

Given these requirements, what tests for boundary conditions can you think of?

Answer 3:

- Phone numbers with an area code of 111, 211, up to 911, 290, 291, etc, 999, 370-379, or 960-969 should throw a Phone-AreaCodeException.

- A phone number with too many digits (in one of each set of number, area code, prefix, number) should throw a Phone-FormatException.

- A phone number with not enough digits (in one of each set) should throw a PhoneFormatException.

- A phone number with illegal characters (spaces, letters, etc.) should throw a PhoneFormatException.

- A phone number that's missing dashes should throw a Phone-FormatException.

- A phone number with multiple dashes should throw a Phone-FormatException.

- A null phone number should throw a PhoneFormatException.

- A file that doesn't exist should throw a MissingOrBadFile-Exception.

- A null filename should also throw that exception.

- An empty file should throw a MissingOrBadFileException.

- A file that's not in the correct format should throw a `Missing-OrBadFileException`.

Exercise 4: *from page 70*

An automatic sewing machine that does embroidery. The class that controls it takes a few basic commands. The coordinates (0,0) represent the lower-left corner of the machine. *x* and *y* increase as you move toward the upper-right corner, whose coordinates are x = `TableSize.Width - 1` and y = `TableSize.Height - 1`.

Coordinates are specified in fractions of centimeters.

```
public void MoveTo(double x, double y);
public void SewTo(double x, double y);
public void SetWorkpieceSize(double width,
                             double height);
public Size WorkpieceSize { get; }
public Size TableSize { get; }
```

There are some real-world constraints that might be interesting: you can't sew thin air, of course, and you can't sew a workpiece bigger than the machine.

Given these requirements, what boundary conditions can you think of?

Answer 4:

- Huge value for one or both coordinates
- Huge value for workpiece size
- Zero or negative value for one or both coordinates
- Zero or negative value for workpiece size
- Coordinates that move off the workpiece
- Workpiece bigger than the table

Exercise 5: *from page 70*

Audio/Video Editing Transport. A class that provides methods to control a VCR or tape deck. There's the notion of a "current position" that lies somewhere between the beginning of tape (BOT) and the end of tape (EOT).

You can ask for the current position and move from there to another given position. *Fast-forward* moves from current position toward EOT by some amount. *Rewind* moves from current position toward BOT by some amount.

When tapes are first loaded, they are positioned at BOT automatically.

```
using System;
public interface AVTransport {
    /// Move the current position ahead by this many
    /// seconds. Fast-forwarding past end-of-tape
    /// leaves the position at end-of-tape
    void FastForward(double seconds);

    /// Move the current position backwards by this
    /// many seconds. Rewinding past zero leaves
    /// the position at zero
    void Rewind(double seconds);

    /// Return current time position in seconds
    double CurrentTimePosition();

    /// Mark the current time position with label
    void MarkTimePosition(String name);

    /// Change the current position to the one
    /// associated with the marked name
    void GotoMark(String name);
}
```

Answer 5:

- Verify that the initial position is BOT.

- Fast forward by some allowed amount (not past end of tape), then rewind by same amount. Should be at initial location.

- Rewind by some allowed amount amount (not past beginning of tape), then fast forward by same amount. Should be at initial location.

- Fast forward past end of tape, then rewind by same amount. Should be before the initial location by an appropriate amount to reflect the fact that you can't advance the location past the end of tape.

- Try the same thing in the other direction (rewind past beginning of tape).

- Mark various positions and return to them after moving the current position around.

- Mark a position and return to it *without* moving in between.

Exercise 6: *from page 71*
Audio/Video Editing Transport, Release 2.0. As above, but now you can position in seconds, minutes, or frames (there are exactly 30 frames per second in this example), and you can move relative to the beginning or the end.

Answer 6: Cross-check results using different units: move in one unit and verify your position using another unit; move forward in one unit and back in another, and so on.

Exercise 7: *from page 134*
Design an interest calculator that calculates the amount of interest based on the number of working days in-between two dates. Use test-first design, and take it one step at a time.

Answer 7: Here's a possible scenario of steps you might take. There is no right answer; this exercise is simply to get you to think about test-first design.

1. Begin by simply calculating the days between any two dates first. The tests might include:
   - Use the same value for first date and last date.
   - Try the normal case where first date < last date.
   - Try the error case where first date > last date.
   - Try dates that span a year boundary (from October 1 2003 to March 1, 2004 for instance).
   - Try dates more than a year apart (from October 1 2003 to December 1, 2006).

2. Next, exclude weekends from the calculation, using the same sorts of tests.

3. Now exclude public and/or corporate holidays. This raises a potentially interesting question: how do you specify holidays? You had to face that issue when writing the tests; do you think doing so improved your interface?

4. Finally, perform the interest calculation itself. You might start off with tests such as:
   - Interest amount should never be negative (an invariant).
   - Interest when first date equals last date should be 0.0.

Index

X

Z

Pragmatic Starter Kit

Version control. **Unit Testing**. **Project Automation**. Three great titles, one objective. To get you up to speed with the essentials for successful project development. Keep your source under control, your bugs in check, and your process repeatable with these three concise, readable books from The Pragmatic Bookshelf.

Visit Us Online

Unit Testing in C# Home Page
pragmaticprogrammer.com/sk/utc
Source code from this book, errata, and other resources. Come give us feedback, too!

Register for Updates
pragmaticprogrammer.com/updates
Be notified when updates and new books become available.

Join the Community
pragmaticprogrammer.com/community
Read our weblogs, join our online discussions, participate in our mailing list, interact with our wiki, and benefit from the experience of other Pragmatic Programmers.

New and Noteworthy
pragmaticprogrammer.com/news
Check out the latest pragmatic developments in the news.

Save on the PDF

Save over 60% on the PDF version of this book. Owning the paper version of this book entitles you to purchase the PDF version for only $7.50 (regularly $20.00). That's a saving of more than 60%. The PDF is great for carrying around on your laptop. It's hyperlinked, has color, and is fully searchable. Buy it now at pragmaticprogrammer.com/coupon

Contact Us

Phone Orders:	1-800-699-PROG (+1 919 847 3884)
Online Orders:	www.pragmaticprogrammer.com/catalog
Customer Service:	orders@pragmaticprogrammer.com
Non-English Versions:	translations@pragmaticprogrammer.com
Pragmatic Teaching:	academic@pragmaticprogrammer.com
Author Proposals:	proposals@pragmaticprogrammer.com